Stretch your KS2 English skills with CGP!

This book is perfect for pupils aged 8-9 who are confident with the Year 4 programme of study for grammar, punctuation and spelling.

It's jam-packed with extra-challenging questions to help them gain a deeper understanding of each topic.

We've also included mixed practice quizzes and a test at the end of the book to help assess where their strengths and weaknesses are!

What CGP is all about

Our sole aim here at CGP is to produce the highest quality books
— carefully written, immaculately presented
and dangerously close to being funny.

Then we work our socks off to get them out to you
— at the cheapest possible prices.

Contents

Grammar

Section 1 — Word Classes
Different Types of Noun 4
Adjectives: Comparative and Superlative....6
Using Adverbs 8
Personal and Possessive Pronouns 10
Determiners 11

Section 2 — Verb Forms
Using Past Tense Verb Forms 12
Using Different Tenses..................14

Section 3 — Phrases and Clauses
Expanded Noun Phrases..................16
Main and Subordinate Clauses 17
Adverbials 18

Section 4 — Using Adverbials
Adverbials of Time 20
Adverbials of Place 22
Adverbials of Cause 24
Adverbials in Fiction & Non-Fiction.............26

Section 5 — Writing Style
Common Error 1: 'Have' or 'Of' 27
Common Error 2: Pronouns with 'and' 28
Common Error 3: Comparatives and Superlatives 29
Verb Agreement and Standard Verb Forms 30

End of Grammar Quiz
End of Grammar Quiz..................32

Punctuation

Section 6 — Sentence Punctuation
Capital Letters..................34
Punctuation for the End of a Sentence 36

Section 7 — Commas and Apostrophes
Commas or Full Stops?..................38
Commas for Lists..................39
Commas with Fronted Adverbials 40
Apostrophes for Contraction 41
Apostrophes for Plural Possession 42
Its / It's and Whose / Who's..................44

Section 8 — Punctuation for Speech
Moving the Reporting Clause..................45
Adding Information to the Reporting Clause 46
Reported and Direct Speech 48

Section 9 — Paragraphs and Layout
Using Paragraphs 50
Paragraphs and Subheadings..................52

End of Punctuation Quiz
End of Punctuation Quiz 54

Contents

Spelling

Section 10 — Prefixes

Prefix: 're'...56
Prefix: 'auto'..57
Negative Prefixes: 'il', 'im', 'in' and 'ir'.........58
Prefixes: 'anti' and 'multi'............................60

Section 11 — Word Endings and Suffixes

Suffixes: 'ous'..61
Suffixes: 'shun' / 'zhun' endings 62
Suffixes: Syllables and
Doubling Consonants..................................64
Word Endings: 'ture', 'sure', 'gue'
and 'que' 66

Section 12 — Confusing Words

Words Containing 'sc' Making An
's' Sound 67
Tricky Homophones 68
Unstressed and Silent Vowels 70
Words from the Year 3/4 Spelling List........71

End of Spelling Quiz

End of Spelling Quiz 74

End of Book Test

End of Book Test 76

Glossary 82
Answers 84

Published by CGP

Written by Joanna Copley and John Svatins

Editors: Eleanor Claringbold, Christopher Lindle, Sam Norman, Hannah Roscoe and Caroline Thomson

Reviewers: Claire Boulter and Maxine Petrie

With thanks to Janet Berkeley, Heather Cowley, Alison Griffin and Holly Robinson for the proofreading.

Thumb illustration used throughout the book © iStock.com
With thanks to Alamy for permission to use the image on page 20.
Page 71 contains public sector information licensed under the Open Government Licence v3.0.
http://www.nationalarchives.gov.uk/doc/open-government-licence/version/3/

ISBN: 978 1 78294 946 6

Clipart from Corel®
Printed by Elanders Ltd, Newcastle upon Tyne.
Based on the classic CGP style created by Richard Parsons.

Text, design, layout and original illustrations © Coordination Group Publications Ltd. (CGP) 2019
All rights reserved.

Photocopying this book is not permitted, even if you have a CLA licence.
Extra copies are available from CGP with next day delivery • 0800 1712 712 • www.cgpbooks.co.uk

Section 1 — Word Classes

Different Types of Noun

Proper nouns are names for specific people, places or things. They need a capital letter. → June, Newcastle

Nouns which are not proper nouns are called common nouns. There are three main types of common noun.

1. Concrete nouns are things you can touch. → leaf, boy, mouse
2. Abstract nouns are things you can't touch. → fear, anger, arrival
3. Collective nouns name a group of things. → swarm of bees

1 Sort the words below into the different noun types by writing them in the boxes.

~~Okavango River~~   ~~wolves~~   ~~freedom~~   ~~Africa~~   ~~courage~~   ~~fleet~~

~~Lake Ngami~~   ~~herd~~   ~~tribe~~   ~~robin~~   ~~flock~~   ~~hunger~~   ~~elephant~~

~~spade~~   ~~metal~~   ~~joy~~   ~~beauty~~   ~~bottle~~   ~~peace~~   ~~Botswana~~

Proper Nouns
Okavango River   Botswana
Africa   Lake Ngami

Common Nouns

Concrete	Abstract	Collective
tribe robin elephant spade metal bottle	freedom courage hunger joy beauty peace	herd wolves flock fleet

② **Complete the three sentences below by adding a noun which makes sense, and match it to the type of noun it is.**

concrete is the feeling of needing a drink.

Abstract is water that falls from clouds.

A *collective* is a large gathering of people.

Collective

Concrete

Abstract

③ **Write two sentences of your own which use an abstract noun. Use a different abstract noun in each sentence.**

1. I have never felt rain on my tounge.
2. I never have touched the Sun and I never will.

④ **Imagine going on a journey with a friend. You come across a group of animals. Write a description of your journey that uses all four noun types.**

Here's an example:
I went to Wales with Aisha. We climbed a mountain and saw a flutter of butterflies. We were amazed by their delicate beauty.

I went to India with my grand Jasleen and we saw a bunch of wolves and I thought they had so much beauty in them. then we had and cake and drink.

"I can identify and use common, proper, collective and abstract nouns."

Adjectives: Comparative and Superlative

Adjectives are words which describe nouns. ⟶ small, beautiful

Comparative adjectives **compare** one thing with another.

The moon is smaller than Earth.

I think Saturn is more beautiful than Mars.

Superlative adjectives say which thing is the **most** or **least**.

Jupiter is the largest planet.

I think Venus is the most interesting planet.

1 Draw lines to match each word or phrase with the correct label.

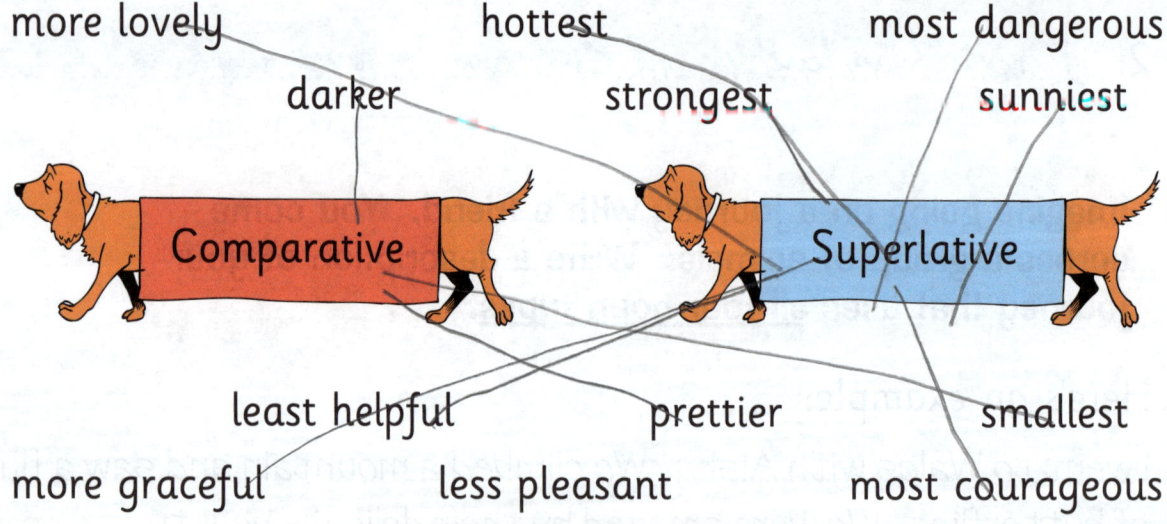

2 Write one sentence using a comparative and one sentence using a superlative.

Comparative: *I do not know the darker person that is in my zoo*

Superlative: ....

3) Complete the table below. The first row has been done for you.

Adjective	Comparative	Superlative
slow	slower	slowest
Happy	happier	happiest
		most annoying
	less expensive	least expensive
		easiest
bright	brighter	brightest
bad		
		best

4) Complete the sentences using a comparative or a superlative of the adjectives in brackets.

(tall) Jeri is ...taller... than I am, but Meg is the ...tallest...

(expensive) This book is .... than that one.

(fussy) Mum's quite fussy but Dad is even ....

(clever) Out of all of us, Josh is the ....

(interesting) York is the .... city I've visited.

(sharp) You need a .... knife than the one you have.

5) Explain what comparatives and superlatives are used for.

....
....

"I can identify and form comparatives and superlatives and use them in my writing."

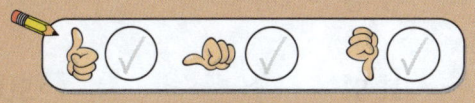

Using Adverbs

Adverbs normally describe verbs:

Sophie thought about it seriously.

'seriously' describes how Sophie thought

Adverbs can also describe adjectives:

Sophie's painting is seriously good!

'seriously' describes how good the painting is

1) Circle the word which the underlined adverb describes, then write whether the word you've circled is a verb or an adjective. The first one has been done for you.

The car is fantastic, but it's <u>shockingly</u> (expensive). ......adjective......

What a <u>brilliantly</u> (funny) story! ......adjectives......

The whole team (played) <u>well</u> today. ......verb......

The best stories are often <u>beautifully</u> (simple). ......adjective......

2) Add an adverb to each sentence below. Some adverbs will need to describe a verb, and some will need to describe an adjective.

It was a ......dreadfully...... dark night.   *You can change 'a' to 'an' if you like.*

Shaun had been acting ......strangely...... all day.

If you speak that ......quickly......, no one will understand.

It's ......rather...... surprising that he arrived so ......early.......

Adverbs can make the adjective they are describing **stronger**:

extremely funny   absolutely dreadful   totally ruined

Or they can make the adjective **weaker**:

slightly amusing   less interesting   faintly annoying

3 Use adverbs from the box to make the adjectives in the sentences below <u>stronger</u> or <u>weaker</u>.

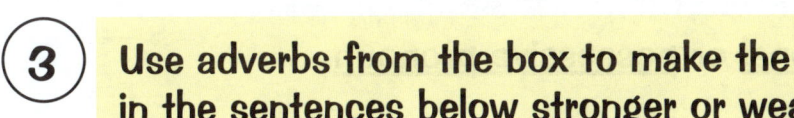

My house has a .....*rather*..... beautiful garden.

She felt .....*fairly*..... sick after eating all that chocolate.

The beach was .....*really*..... clean, and there was no litter.

She is having a .....*somewhat*..... difficult time at the moment.

The weather was .....*much*..... worse today than yesterday.

Climbing that tree was a .....*pretty*..... dangerous thing to do.

4 Write two sentences of your own that use <u>adverbs</u> to make the adjectives <u>stronger</u> or <u>weaker</u>.

Stronger: *When we travel to Butlins the car journey is extremely long.*

Weaker: *Last week my sister was less annoying than usual.*

"I can identify sentence adverbs and use adverbs to make adjectives stronger or weaker."

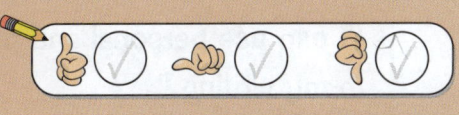

Personal and Possessive Pronouns

Personal pronouns replace nouns. → I, you, he, she, it, we, they

Possessive pronouns show who owns something. → mine, yours, his, hers, its, ours, theirs

1) Fill in the gaps with a personal or possessive pronoun.

"That cake is ...mine... and this cake is ...yours... ," she said.

Ella said ...she... would read my story if I read ...hers... .

"This hedge of ...ours... is too high," Joe said. "...I... need a ladder."

The dogs thought the food was ...theirs..., so ...they... ate it!

Ned and I said the ball was ...ours... and ...we... wanted it back.

2) Imagine you and a friend argued about who owned a book. Describe what happened using personal and possessive pronouns.

I had a book called cinderella and my friend borrowed it. She asked if she was allowed to keep it. The next second it was gone. I shouted at her and exclaimed it was mine but she said it was hers.

3) Why does the underlined pronoun make the sentence below unclear?

Laura told her friend that <u>she</u> couldn't go to the party.

....

....

"I can use personal and possessive pronouns in my writing."

Section 1 — Word Classes © CGP — not to be photocopied

Determiners

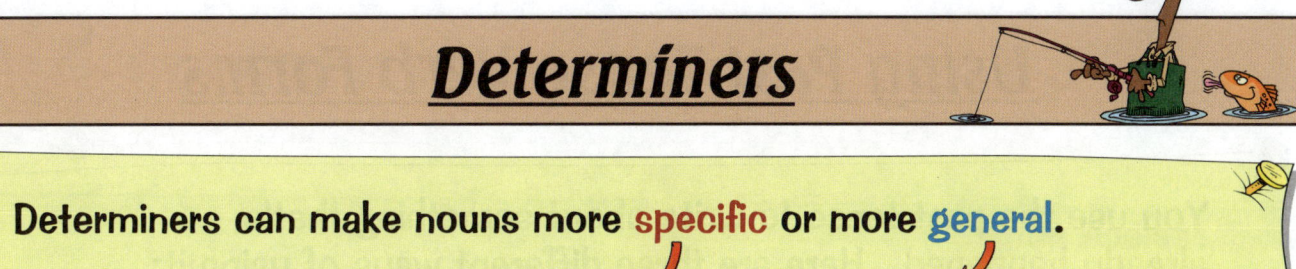

Determiners can make nouns more **specific** or more **general**.

the car, these books, my arm, seven seconds

a bike, some pens, a few leaves

1) Choose a suitable <u>determiner</u> for each space.

I tried to pick ..**an**.. apple from ..**the**.. highest branch but I fell to ..**the**.. ground. I ripped ..**a**.. hole in my jeans but ..**these**.. jeans are old. ..**Seven**.. apples on the tree were fine, but ..**one**.. apple had maggots in it.

2) Fussy Phil and Easy Ernie have mixed up their shopping lists. Sort the items in the box so that those with <u>specific</u> determiners go in <u>Phil's list</u> and the items with <u>general</u> determiners go into <u>Ernie's list</u>.

some pencils ✓	many biscuits ✓	a newspaper ✓
those pens ✓	The Daily Blurb ✓	a few doughnuts ✓
Arthur's cakes ✓	lots of pears ✓	three apples ✓

<u>Fussy Phil</u>
many biscuits
those pens, the daily blurb
Arthur's cakes, three apples

<u>Easy Ernie</u>
some pencils, a newspaper
a few doughnuts, lots of pears
many biscuits

"I can identify and use determiners."

Section 2 — Verb Forms

Using Past Tense Verb Forms

You use the past tense to write about something that's **already happened**. Here are three different ways of using it:

I walked to school. ← **Simple past** — the verb is always just one word, often ending –ed.

I was walking along the road for over an hour. ← **Past progressive** — made of 'was' or 'were' and an 'ing' form of a verb.

I have walked along this road before. ← **Present perfect** — made of 'have' or 'has' and a past tense form of a verb.

1) Draw a line to match each group of words to the **correct label**.

she has answered		we were deciding
you were thinking	simple past	he has noticed
he was building		I was guarding
they remembered	past progressive	you mentioned
I have caught		they have learned
we promised	present perfect	she imagined

2) Write one sentence for **each of the three verb forms**. Don't use any of the verbs shown in Question 1.

simple past ....

past progressive ....

present perfect ....

3

Write two sentences that each use two different past tense verb forms. Use the verbs in the box to help you.

Here's an example:
I <u>was washing</u> my bike when I <u>heard</u> the crash.

The past tense verb forms are underlined.

| cut   drop   swing   grab   jump   see   watch   hurry   smash   run |

1. ....

2. ....

4

Fill the gaps in the story below with a suitable past tense form of each verb in brackets so that it makes sense. Count how many times you have used each form and put your answers in the boxes at the end.

'I'm going out,' (say).................... Dad. 'I (make)....................

you a salad for lunch. Enjoy!'

After lunch, we (tidy).................... and (clean)....................

the kitchen. I (think).................... about building my model

plane, but Jaz (want).................... to go out in the garden.

We (argue).................... about it, when there (be)....................

a knock on the door. The postman (stand).................... there

with a package.

'I nearly (break).................... my back

carrying this,' he (puff).................... .

If you can, compare your answers with a partner. If some of your verb forms don't match, discuss why.

Simple past: ☐   Past progressive: ☐   Present perfect: ☐

"I can identify and use different forms of the past tense."

Using Different Tenses

Using different tenses in your writing helps you to explain to the reader the order of what happens when.

1 Number these sentences so they are in a sensible order. Use the underlined verb forms in each sentence to help you.

Start by reading through all the sentences. Before putting any numbers in, you could jot down whether you think each sentence is nearer the start or the end of the story.

Tomorrow we <u>are going to make</u> posters for the play. ☐

On the morning of the trip, we <u>dressed</u> in war-time clothes, so we <u>looked</u> like children in the 1940s. ☐

Last week, we <u>went</u> on a theatre trip to see a play. [1]

Since our trip, we <u>have written</u> about what it <u>was</u> like for children to be evacuated to the countryside. ☐

The play <u>was</u> about children being evacuated in the war. ☐

We <u>were looking forward</u> to the trip, as we <u>had never seen</u> a play about the war before. ☐

I <u>thought</u> it <u>was</u> quite sad, but I really <u>enjoyed</u> it. ☐

Section 2 — Verb Forms

In your writing, it is important not to change tenses **without a reason**.

My class went to see a play. We are feeling very excited. We get on the coach and the driver took us to the theatre. ✗

This text mixes past and present tenses.

This text is all in the past tense.

My class went to see a play. We were feeling very excited. We got on the coach and the driver took us to the theatre. ✓

2) In this diary entry, some of the <u>verb forms</u> are in the <u>wrong tense</u>. Cross out forms that are wrong and write the correct versions above.

Dear Diary,

Yesterday, I ~~go~~ ⁽went⁾ to karate after school. I enjoy it, but my friend Sam was hating it and said it is boring. We walked home together and I carry his bag because he's really tired.

3) Write your own <u>diary entry</u> using a variety of tenses. Only change tenses when there's a <u>reason</u> to do so.

Yesterday, I ....

....

....

....

....

"I can use tenses correctly in my writing."

Section 3 — Phrases and Clauses

Expanded Noun Phrases

Expanded noun phrases are made by adding extra words, phrases and clauses to a noun. So instead of just saying 'jam', you might say:

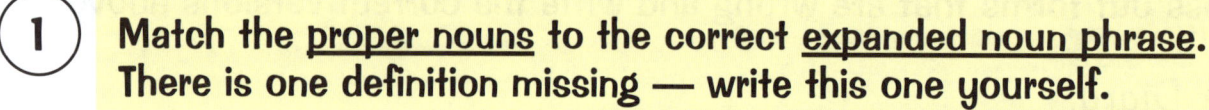

that — determiner
delicious — adjective
raspberry — noun
in the fridge — preposition phrase

Expanded noun phrases are useful for defining exactly what something is, and also for adding detail to make your writing more interesting.

1) Match the proper nouns to the correct expanded noun phrase. There is one definition missing — write this one yourself.

- 10 Downing Street
- Irish Sea
- Loch Ness
- Pennines

- a body of water separating Britain and Ireland
- the official home of the Prime Minister of the United Kingdom
- a range of hills sometimes called the 'backbone of England'
- ....
  ....

2) Think of your own proper noun and write it in the box. Then write an expanded noun phrase to define it.

[ ] ....
     ....

"I can use expanded noun phrases in definitions and descriptions."

Main and Subordinate Clauses

A main clause tells you the key things that are happening in a sentence. A subordinate clause gives extra information.

Sentences can contain more than one of each type of clause.

subordinate clause   main clause

When Jan reached home, she put the key in the door but the lock was broken.

main clause

1 Underline any <u>subordinate clauses</u> and circle any <u>main clauses</u> in the sentences below.

Subordinate clauses often start with words like 'because', 'when', 'if', 'after', 'before', 'although', 'since' and 'until'. These are called <u>subordinating conjunctions</u>.

I can help you if you'd like me to.

After it had stopped raining, I went outside for a stroll.

Suki really likes cycling but she can't stand jogging.

Although they loved travelling, they decided to stay at home until Bill was in better health.

2 Join these <u>three clauses</u> in any order into one sentence by adding <u>conjunctions</u>. Make at least one of the clauses a <u>subordinate clause</u>.

Larry had to wait / Hayley was late / there were no buses

....

....

"I can identify and use main and subordinate clauses."

Adverbials

Adverbials tell you how, when, where or how often something happens. An adverbial can be:

an adverb → An ash tree fell spectacularly.

a phrase → An ash tree fell last night.

a subordinate clause → When the storm came, an ash tree fell.

When an adverbial comes at the start of a sentence, it needs a comma after it.

1 Draw a line to match each group of words to the correct label.

before school		the phone rang
Jack came in	Main Clause	because he missed her
outside the door		suddenly
we pretended to read	Adverbial	we got a surprise
with a huge crash		before she arrived

2 <u>Underline</u> the adverbial in each sentence below, and then write whether it is an <u>adverb</u>, a <u>phrase</u> or a <u>subordinate clause</u>.

The climber rested for a few moments. → ....

I do ballet at the church hall. → ....

Although we were tired, we couldn't stop. → ....

Luckily, I found a five pound note. → ....

They fell asleep after they'd eaten. → ....

Section 3 — Phrases and Clauses

③ **Add an adverbial of the type shown in green to the sentences below.**

adverb ➔ .... I had to go shopping.

phrase ➔ I had to go shopping ....

subordinate clause ➔

...., I had to go shopping.

④ **Imagine that you are escaping from a dinosaur. Complete the paragraph below describing your escape using different adverbials. Underline all the adverbials you have used.**

I knew that the dinosaur had not eaten that day,

so I ran ....

....

....

....

....

....

⑤ **Explain in your own words what an adverbial is.**

....

....

"I can identify adverbials and understand how they add information to sentences."

Section 4 — Using Adverbials

Adverbials of Time

You can use adverbials in your writing to show **when** one thing happens in relation to another. Adverbials of time are in red.

> Before I went to school, I couldn't read. As soon as I got there, I started to learn, and now I can read very well.

This makes your writing clearer and helps it to flow better.

1) Underline the <u>adverbials of time</u> in this passage.

   As soon as the sun rose, Tai got out of bed. He dressed, and then ran downstairs. The day before, there had been very little food in the cupboard for breakfast, but later on, Gemma had come in with a big piece of lamb, and that night they had feasted. This morning, Tai was expecting there to be cold meat and bread. But when he opened the cupboard, it was empty. The food had gone.
   'I'm sorry,' said Gemma. 'After you'd gone to bed, the neighbours came by. They hadn't had anything to eat since yesterday morning, so I gave them our food. We can always get more tomorrow.'
   'But I'm hungry NOW!' said Tai, desperately. 'We can't go on like this, wondering every day whether there will be food soon.'

2) Write down as many other <u>adverbials of time</u> as you can.

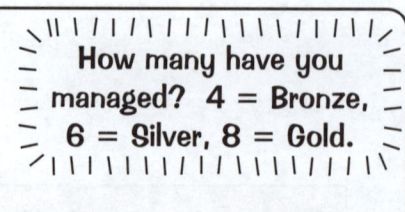

How many have you managed? 4 = Bronze, 6 = Silver, 8 = Gold.

3 Make these short sentences into longer sentences by linking the events by time. The order of events is up to you. The first one has been done for you.

He saw the car crash. He walked home.

While he was walking home from school, he saw the car crash.

Her alarm sounded. She jumped out of bed.

....

The cat ran away. The dog barked. The cat hissed.

....

We sailed into the harbour. The wind rose. There was a loud crack. The mast broke. The sails fell on the deck. We could not see anything. We bumped the harbour wall.

....

....

....

....

4 Add a sentence including at least one adverbial of time to the sailing story from Question 3. Underline all the adverbials of time you use.

....

....

"I can use adverbials of time to improve my writing."

Adverbials of Place

 Adverbials of place tell the reader where the action of your sentence takes place.

> Beneath an ancient oak, Jamal sat on a rounded stone and pondered.

These adverbials of place paint a picture in the mind of the reader, and make your writing more vivid.

1) Write down an adverbial to show the position of each thing in the picture.

the bear: ....

the girls: ....

the dwarf: ....

the town: ....

2) Now combine your adverbials from Question 1 with some action. Write two sentences about the picture which contain both verbs and adverbials of place.

1. ....

....

2. ....

....

Section 4 — Using Adverbials

3) Add an <u>adverbial of place</u> to each sentence below. The first one has been done for you.

<u>Stretched out upon heaps of gold</u>..............., the dragon brooded.

...., the lonely ship sailed onwards.

The spy lurked silently ....

...., the fairy danced in the moonlight.

The cheetah sprinted ....

...., the fans started to gather.

He sat quietly ....

4) Choose one of the settings given below. Imagine you are there. Write a passage with <u>adverbials of place</u> to describe the landscape.

| an undersea garden full of coral, weed and sea creatures | an abandoned mine full of shadows and broken machinery |

....
....
....
....
....
....

"I can use adverbials of place to improve my writing."

Adverbials of Cause

You can use **adverbials of cause** to explain **why** something happens.

Because of the rain, we stayed indoors.

She was rude to me once. **Therefore,** I do not wish to see her.

Adverbials of cause help to make your writing more **reasoned** and **logical**, and help it to **flow better**.

1 Underline the **adverbial of cause** in each of the sentences below.

Since it is written in French, I don't really understand it.

I don't want to try the big trampoline in case I fall off it.

As you are so keen, I'll let you have a go.

He couldn't drive to work due to problems with his car.

Put the dog on the lead now, please, because she might run away.

2 Complete each sentence below with an **adverbial of cause**.

I stayed at home ....

We ought to go shopping ....

...., we will have to postpone our trip.

...., we should have a picnic.

Section 4 — Using Adverbials © CGP — not to be photocopied

3 Complete the sentences below about what you plan to do this weekend. Each sentence should contain an <u>adverbial of cause</u>.

On Saturday, ...,

because ....

Since ....,

....

Due to ....,

....

4 Rewrite the passage below, making it flow better by adding <u>adverbials of cause</u>.

> Kie and the dog were bored. It was raining. They couldn't watch TV. Mum had hidden the remote. Kie decided to teach the dog to walk on its hind legs. The dog got cross. A vase was broken.

Think about <u>why</u> all these events may have happened.

As it had been raining all day, Kie and the dog were really bored.

....

....

....

....

"I can use adverbials of cause to improve my writing."

Adverbials in Fiction & Non-Fiction

Using adverbials can help to make the language in your fiction and non-fiction writing rich and informative.

1) Write the opening of a story set in a supermarket. Use plenty of adverbials to add detail to your writing. Underline all the adverbials.

....

....

....

....

....

....

2) Explain a few of the rules of your school to a new pupil. Use adverbials to make it clear exactly when, where and why the rules apply. Underline all the adverbials.

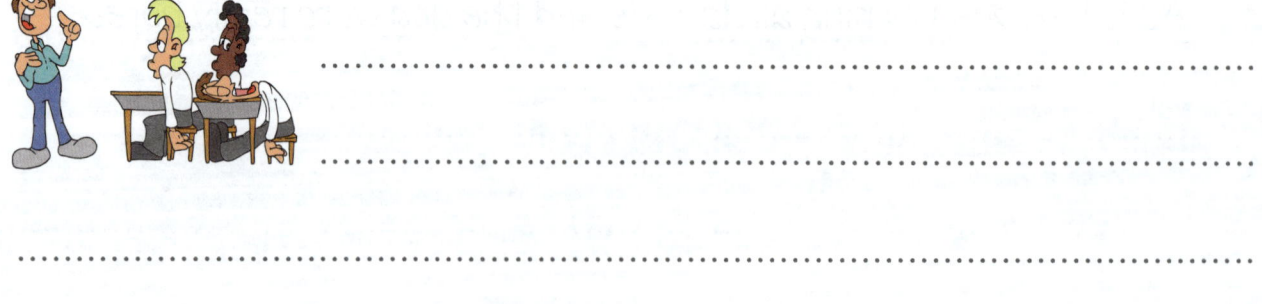

"I can use adverbials effectively in my fiction and non-fiction writing."

Section 4 — Using Adverbials

Section 5 — Writing Style

Common Error 1: 'Have' or 'Of'

Sometimes people get 'have' and 'of' confused. For example:

| could have ✓ | should have ✓ | would have ✓ | might have ✓ |

| could of ✗ | should of ✗ | would of ✗ | might of ✗ |

In written speech, you can use this shortened form of 'have':

| could've | should've | would've | might've |

In general though, you should write them as two words.

1) Cross out and correct the sentences below which use 'have' and 'of' incorrectly.

I might of known.

Have course you should!

I'd never of thought of that.

They didn't go, but maybe they should of.

"You should've seen it!" he said, laughing.

2) Write your own sentences about something you did recently which might have turned out differently. Include 'could have', 'would have' and 'should have'.

....

....

....

"I can avoid errors using 'have' and 'of'."

Common Error 2: Pronouns with 'and'

It can be hard to know which pronoun to use after the word 'and'.

Molly and me will go to the concert. ✗ ← You can't say 'me will go'. It's 'I will go'.

Molly and I will go to the concert. ✓

Chris gave Molly and I his tickets. ✗ ← You can't say 'Chris gave... I'. It's 'Chris gave... me'.

Chris gave Molly and me his tickets. ✓

You also need to be careful with the pronouns 'he/him' and 'she/her'.

Me and him got on well. ✗

He and I got on well. ✓ ← It's generally considered better style to put 'I' last. So it's 'He and I' rather than 'I and he'.

1) Tick all the sentences which use <u>pronouns</u> correctly.

☐ David and I will do it.   ☐ David and me will do it.
☐ You can trust David and me.   ☐ You can trust David and I.
☐ I think me and him should go.   ☐ I think he and I should go.

2) Correct any mistakes with <u>pronouns</u> in the passage below.

Benji and me decided to sneak out. It was a bit naughty of my brother and I, but we risked it anyway. Rachael spotted us leaving but didn't say anything. Her and me have always got on.

"I can use the correct pronouns with 'and'."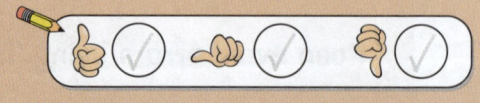

Common Error 3: Comparatives and Superlatives

Some adjectives don't work in the comparative or superlative form.

> Science is my most favourite lesson. ✗

'Favourite' already means 'most liked', so you don't need 'most' in front of it. It should be 'my favourite lesson'.

It's not just adjectives that can already imply a comparison or superlative:

> I prefer carrots more than peas. ✗

'Prefer' already means 'like more'. It should be 'I prefer carrots to peas', or 'I like carrots more than peas.'

1 Explain what is wrong with each example below. Write a <u>corrected version</u> in the green box.

the most funniest joke →

a more inferior product →

the mountain's highest summit →

the most ideal place →

"I can avoid double comparatives and superlatives."

Verb Agreement and Standard Verb Forms

Verbs sometimes need to change according to who or what is doing the action. This is called verb agreement.

Singular noun (just one cow)...

A cow walk**s** across the field.

... means this verb needs an 's'.

Plural noun (more than one cow)...

Two cows walk across the field.

... means this verb has no 's'.

1) Draw a line to connect the start of each sentence to an end. Make sure the verb form matches the noun.

You can make your sentences as weird as you like.

A bear — drinks tea.
The elephants — meet at midnight.
My Nan — eat sugar-cane.
The athlete — runs marathons.
Three sisters — catches the salmon.

2) Underline the verbs in the passage below which do not agree with the nouns. Then rewrite the passage so that they do agree.

Water freeze at 0 °C and become ice. This frozen water floats on

....

liquid water. Most other substances does not behave in this way;

....

their frozen form sink in the liquid form. When you heat water to

....

100 °C, bubbles forms and water turn into a gas.

....

Section 5 — Writing Style

To write in Standard English, you need to avoid non-Standard verb forms like these:

I done my homework, then I seen my friend.

In Standard English this would be:

I did my homework, then I saw my friend.

3 Underline each non-standard verb form and then draw a line to match it to its standard form.

We was	I'm not	They been	You saw
I've gone	I ain't	We were	She did
You seen	They went	She done	I've went

4 Cross out any non-standard verb forms and write the correct standard form above.

 were
We ~~was~~ on our way to the shops when we seen a horse galloping down the road. It had ran away from its owner. I begun to panic. Mum was fearless though and ran to catch it. We put a scarf round its neck to hold it and given it a carrot, but while we was waiting for its owner, it done a wee over Mum's shoes.

"I can make verbs agree with their nouns, and identify and correct non-Standard verb forms."

End of Grammar Quiz

1) Put the nouns below into the box with the correct heading. Add capital letters if necessary.

courage   gate   fear   monday   crowd   flock
london   carpet   ferrari   oak   trust   tribe

Concrete

Proper

Abstract

Collective

2 marks

2) Write whether the underlined words in the sentences below are a determiner, a pronoun or an adverb.

Can you donate <u>any</u> clothes?   ....

Danny wants <u>me</u> to tie his laces.   ....

His cooking is <u>really</u> terrible.   ....

1 mark

3) Draw lines to join these sentences to the verb form being used.

Samir was running in an obstacle race.   simple past

Who has eaten my biscuit?

I saw your friend in town.   present perfect

They weren't helping us.   past progressive

1 mark

4) Circle the possessive pronouns in the sentences below.

Are these sunglasses yours? I think I have lost mine.

1 mark

5 **Underline the subordinate clause in each sentence.**

The jewels were stolen <u>before I could raise the alarm</u>.

<u>Once the weather improved</u>, we went ahead with the barbecue and had a great time.

1 mark

6 **Write in the correct comparative or superlative adjective.**

more happy	most strange	most bad
....	....	....
happier	strangest	worst

most pretty	most boring	more good
....	....	....
prettiest	most boring	better

2 marks

7 **Underline the adverbials and say whether they show time, place or cause.**

<u>As it was raining</u>, the swimming pool was packed. .... (cause)

The tiny lizard lounged <u>on the side of the wall</u>. .... (place)

1 mark

8 **Choose 'I' or 'me' to complete each sentence.**

Dad built a slide in the garden for my sister and .... (me) .

Izzy and .... (I) solved the puzzle together.

My brother and .... (I) made a terrible mess.

1 mark

I scored ☐ out of 10.

Section 6 — Sentence Punctuation

Capital Letters

Capital letters are used for all proper nouns — the names of particular places, people, dates, events or organisations.

Devon Fire Service ← Although 'fire' and 'service' are common nouns, altogether this phrase makes up a proper noun.

With words like 'mum', 'mother', 'dad' and 'father', if there is a determiner there (the, a, my, his, your) you will not need a capital. → My dad can't come.

If there is no determiner, you will need a capital. → I helped Dad.

1 Rewrite the sentences with the necessary capital letters.

on valentine's day, I received a card addressed to mr snuffles.

....

....

the book dad read was about the royal air force.

....

....

in the spring of 1774, the british explorer james cook arrived at easter island in the pacific ocean.

 The names of seasons don't need a capital letter.

....

....

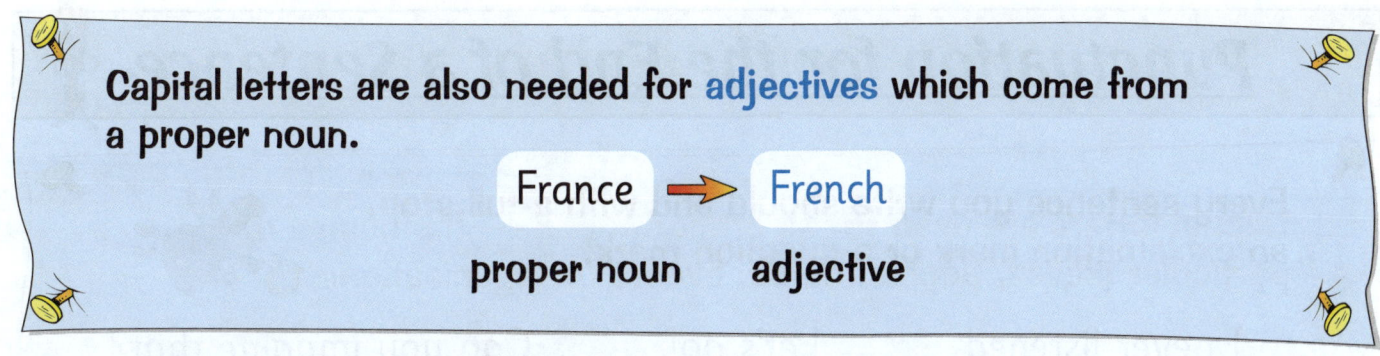

Capital letters are also needed for adjectives which come from a proper noun.

France → French

proper noun   adjective

2 Write the missing adjective or proper noun in each pairing below. Then write two pairs of proper nouns and adjectives.

Scotland → Scottish   .... → Shakespearean

Italy → .... → Victorian

Denmark → .... → Martian

Elizabeth → .... → Israeli

Rome → .... → ....

Canada → .... → ....

3 Write your own sentence which includes a proper noun and an adjective which comes from a proper noun.

....

....

....

"I can use capital letters for proper nouns and adjectives which come from proper nouns."

Punctuation for the End of a Sentence

Every sentence you write should end with a full stop, an exclamation mark or a question mark.

I never listened.   Let's go!   Can you imagine that?

1 Complete the passage below using each word from the box once only.

statements   questions   commands   exclamations

.... should always end with a question mark.

You use .... when you're telling someone what to do. These can end with a full stop or an exclamation mark, depending on how forceful or urgent they are.

.... are sentences like, "What a nice day it is!"

.... should end with a full stop, unless they show a lot of emotion, in which case they can end with an exclamation mark.

2 Add the correct punctuation mark to complete each sentence below.

I have two sisters ☐   Pass the sugar please, Milly ☐

What a pain you are ☐   I asked him a question ☐

What did he say ☐   Could you help me, please ☐

Look out ☐   It was so amazing ☐

3 **Rewrite the passage below, adding the correct sentence punctuation.**

i'm so jealous what an amazing holiday i've never been to america did you go by plane where did you stay

....

....

....

....

4 **Imagine an alien has landed on Earth and wants to understand how we write. Answer his questions below.**

Make sure you punctuate your answers correctly to demonstrate that you know what you're talking about.

Why do Earthlings put dots and squiggles at the end of sentences?

....

....

....

Why are there 3 different shapes to show the end of the sentence?

....

....

....

....

"I can correctly punctuate statements, commands, questions and exclamations."

Section 7 — Commas and Apostrophes

Commas or Full Stops?

When you write two main clauses and no conjunction, they usually need to be separated by a **full stop**.

> Everybody loved the cakes I baked. They were very popular.

When a sentence starts with a subordinate clause, it should be separated from the main clause by a **comma**.

> When you cross the road, make sure you look both ways.

1) Add <u>one comma</u> and <u>one full stop</u> to each piece of text. Cross out and correct any letters which should be <u>capital letters</u>.

Before we had dinner we played in the park it was 8 o'clock by the time we ate.

As the spectators applauded Gary struggled to reach the bench that last tackle had really hurt him.

2) Correct the passage below by adding <u>full stops</u> and <u>commas</u>. Cross out and correct any letters which should be <u>capital letters</u>.

it was the day of the athletics competition each day after she had finished school Milly had practised on the field near her house now she was ready before she left she checked her bag one more time everything was there

"I can separate main clauses with a full stop and use commas after subordinate clauses."

Commas for Lists

In lists, commas separate the items from each other. Here's an example:

Kelly found sweet wrappers, a teddy bear, a broken watch, the remains of a pork pie and a pack of cards inside the giant's pocket.

There is no need for a comma before 'and'.

1) Complete the lists below by adding four items to each one.

The greengrocer's colourful display included a yellow lemon,

....

....

At the alphabetical party, there was an artist from Albania,

....

....

2) Use commas to write all the words in the box as a shopping list of four items. Then use the same words to make a list of five items.

| chocolate   biscuits   ice   cream   fruit   juice |

Please buy the following four items: ....

....

Please buy the following five items: ....

....

"I can use commas to separate items in a list."

Commas with Fronted Adverbials

When the adverbial comes at the start of the sentence, you will need a comma before the main clause.

At the fair, I went on a scary rollercoaster.

Look back at pages 18-19 for a reminder on adverbials.

If the adverbial comes after the main clause, no comma is needed.

I went on a scary rollercoaster at the fair.

1) Add a comma after each fronted adverbial in the sentences below.

In the cupboard a family of mice feasted on biscuit crumbs.

With an angry yell my sister snatched back her lollipop.

Before the film had started the boys had eaten all their popcorn.

2) Change the position of the adverbial so that it starts the sentence.

Sophia scored the winning goal with a mighty shot.

....

....

My guinea pig squeals whenever I give her parsley.

....

....

"I can use commas after fronted adverbials."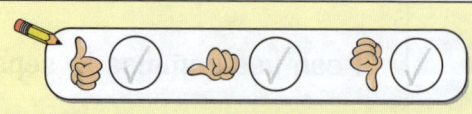

Apostrophes for Contraction

Apostrophes can show contraction. This is where letters are removed.

they are → they're

Sometimes the word changes a bit though.

will not → won't

Be careful — some contractions can stand for more than one thing.

I'd seen it before. (I had)   I'd go there again. (I would)

1 Circle the word where the apostrophe has been correctly placed.

weren't / werent' / were'nt

do'esnt / doesn't / does'nt

they're / they're / the'yre

have'nt / hav'ent / haven't

2 Write the long form of each contraction after the sentence.

Who'd been in my room? ....

They'd soon be at their destination. ....

Nobody's got any money. ....

There's about half a glass left. ....

3 Write your own sentence that includes at least two contractions.

....
....

"I can work out the meaning of a contraction from its context, and can use contractions in sentences."

Apostrophes for Plural Possession

Apostrophes for possession show who owns what.
The position of the apostrophe can change the meaning.

The dog's bowl   The dogs' bowl

This is the bowl of one dog.   This is the bowl of more than one dog.

1 Rewrite these phrases using an apostrophe for possession.

The staffroom of the teachers .... The teachers' staffroom

The tusks of the elephants ....

The tracks of the animals ....

The hive of the bees ....

2 Read each phrase and put a tick next to the appropriate description.

The cars' lights
- [ ] The lights of one car
- [ ] The lights of more than one car

Fergus's school
- [ ] The school of one boy called Fergus
- [ ] The school of more than one Fergus

The foxes' den
- [ ] The den of one fox
- [ ] The den of more than one fox

The fly's wings
- [ ] The wings of one fly
- [ ] The wings of more than one fly

The bus's seats
- [ ] The seats of one bus
- [ ] The seats of more than one bus

Section 7 — Commas and Apostrophes

In these examples, the apostrophe goes **before the 's'** because the word is **already a plural**.

→ the children's toys

→ people's opinions

3 Circle the correct uses of the apostrophe to show <u>plural possession</u>.

men's ties   mens' ties

girls's bikes   girls' bikes

sheeps' wool   sheep's wool

mices' food   mice's food

team's field   teams' field

wolfs's howls   wolves' howls

4 Use an apostrophe to show <u>who owns what</u> in these pictures.

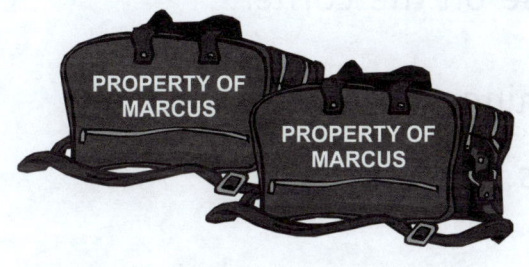

....

....

....

....

"I can place apostrophes correctly to show plural possession."

Its / It's and Whose / Who's

For tricky words like its / it's and whose / who's, the spelling that has an apostrophe usually shows contraction, not possession.

It's time to go home.
Contraction of 'it is'

The dog played with its stick.
Possession

Who's there?
Contraction of 'who is'

Whose keys are these?
Possession

1 Choose its or it's to fill the gaps in the sentences below.

We found a cat. I don't know .... name but .... probably from the house on the corner.

If .... too late to go swimming, can you get out my bike and pump up .... tyres?

The car failed .... test and now .... being scrapped.

2 Choose whose or who's to fill the gaps in the sentences below.

I think I know .... shoes are in the bush, but I don't know .... responsible for putting them there.

"................ been to Paris?" asked the teacher.

"................ going there this summer?"

I don't know .... story to believe.

"I can make the right choice when using its / it's and whose / who's."

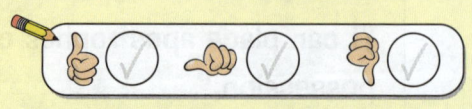

Section 8 — Punctuation for Speech

Moving the Reporting Clause

A **reporting clause** can go at the **beginning** or **end** of a sentence.

Jasmin said, "Why are you digging in the sand?"

"Why are you digging in the sand?" said Jasmin.

The reporting clause can also go in the **middle** of the sentence. Breaking the sentence can make the dialogue **more interesting**.

"Why on Earth," said Jasmin, "are you digging in the sand?"

You need **commas** before and after the reporting clause when it's breaking up a sentence of dialogue.

1) Rewrite the sentence below with the reporting clause in the **middle**. Make sure you punctuate the sentence correctly.

"I do like Mrs Oxley but she can be a bit fierce," he said.

....

....

2) Write your own sentence which has the reporting clause in the **middle**.

....

....

....

"I can correctly punctuate a sentence which has a reporting clause in the middle."

© CGP — not to be photocopied

Adding Information to the Reporting Clause

You can add **adverbs** to a reporting clause to show how something is being said.

"Don't be shy," said Robyn gently. "It's ok."

There's a full stop here because the reporting clause is between two sentences of speech.

You can also add other **adverbials** to show what the speaker is doing as they're speaking.

"Don't be shy," said Robyn, patting the kitten on the head. "It's ok."

Longer adverbials in the reporting clause need this extra **comma**.

1) Choose an **adverb** from the box to add to the reporting clause. Make sure you add any **missing commas** or **full stops**.

> sadly   softly   furiously   harshly   later
> today   suddenly   indoors   often   daily
> next   angrily   cheerfully   happily   wearily

"Stop it," said Hanna .... "It's not fair to tease."

"Do I have to go to school?" Andy enquired ....

"I'd quite like to go home," said Jill .... "I'm tired."

"OK, what can I do for you?" asked Shruti ....

John muttered .... "I've had enough of this."

"What a mess!" Mum exclaimed .... "Clear it up!"

Jin said .... "I wonder if it'll ever look clean."

2 Add a reporting clause with <u>extra information</u> into the middle of the examples of speech shown below. Be careful to use the correct punctuation. The first one has been done for you.

"I'm not going to the party, and you can't make me."

"I'm not going to the party," said Ethan shakily, hiding behind the door, "and you can't make me."

"Wherever we go, I think we will always be the best of friends."

....

....

"There are old mines from the war on this beach. Be careful!"

....

....

"I've always liked adventure, but of course not everyone does."

....

....

3 Rewrite the sentences and add all the correct <u>speech punctuation</u>.

> Can we go straight down to the beach asked Tash dumping her bag on the bed I really want to go swimming

....

....

....

"I can punctuate direct speech correctly when information is added to the reporting clause."

Reported and Direct Speech

Reported speech tells you what someone said.

 Mum told me that she was going shopping today.

In direct speech, this would be:

 Mum said, "I am going shopping today."

When you switch from reported to direct speech, you often need to change the pronoun and the tense. So 'she was' changes to 'I am'.

1 Match up each example of reported speech below with the appropriate example written as direct speech.

Reported	Direct
She told me she was cold.	She exclaimed that it was a nuisance.
"Come here, please," I said.	"Is your dog very old?" I said.
"What a nuisance!" she said.	I told her to come over to me.
She said she was too tired to go.	"I don't like milk," he said.
I asked if her dog was very old.	"I'm too tired to go," she said.
He said that he didn't like milk.	"Put your stuff away!" said Mum.
Mum told me to put my stuff away.	"I'm cold," she cried.

Section 8 — Punctuation for Speech

2 Change the reported speech to direct speech. Look for the words that are actually spoken. Remember to use the correct punctuation. The first one has been done for you.

The owner told the vet that her horse hadn't been well.

"My horse hasn't been well," the owner said to the vet.

Raj told me that he much preferred playing rugby to football.

....

Megan replied that she couldn't do that maths work.

....

3 Rewrite the passage of reported speech below so it's in direct speech.

> Mary told Nenad that she didn't mind walking, but she preferred to get a bus. Nenad answered that there weren't any buses going to the beach. Mary replied that she hoped there would be an ice cream van there, as she wanted a choc ice.

....
....
....
....
....
....

"I can recognise reported and direct speech, and change one to the other."

Section 9 — Paragraphs and Layout

Using Paragraphs

You can use **TIPTOP** to help you decide when to **start a new paragraph**.

TIPTOP stands for **TIME**, **PLACE**, **TOPIC** or **PERSON SPEAKING**.

Whenever any of those things **change**, you need to start a new paragraph.

1) Show where the paragraph breaks should be in the passage below by adding in two lines (like this //). Write down in the margin on the left why there needs to be a new paragraph (e.g. 'new time', 'new place').

"Where did he go?" gasped Josh, stopping suddenly. "I can't see which street he went down!" "I'm not sure," Ellie said, just as exhausted as Josh. "I think we're going to have to split up. You grab his collar, and I'll take his lead. At least that way we'll each have something to hold him with." It had seemed like an easy thing to do at first, offering to dog-sit Mr Knight's new puppy while he went out. He hadn't had it very long, and he didn't want to leave it alone all day. Josh and Ellie needed some pocket money, too. At the cricket club, Mr Knight was busy talking to the team captain.

2) Write three paragraphs about a <u>day out</u> you've had recently. It could be a school trip or a trip you made from home.

Make sure you organise your paragraphs. For example, you might write one about where you went and why, one about the journey, and one about what you did when you got there.

....
....
....
....
....
....
....
....
....
....
....
....
....
....

3) Explain why it's important to <u>arrange</u> your writing in <u>paragraphs</u>.

....
....
....

"I understand when and why new paragraphs are needed, and I can write in paragraphs."

Paragraphs and Subheadings

Subheadings help to divide up a text to show what each section is about.

Usually fiction doesn't have subheadings. They would break the text up too much and distract your reader. A change of paragraph is enough to show the story is moving on.

Subheadings are more common in non-fiction texts. You want to break the text up, so your reader can quickly find the information they want.

1 Match each type of text to one of the clouds to show whether or not it should have <u>subheadings</u> to make the information <u>clearer</u>.

A letter to the head teacher, complaining about homework

A note to your friend about a party

A recount of a school trip

NO SUBHEADINGS

A newspaper report

A funny poem

A recipe for scones

An adventure story

SUBHEADINGS

A fairy tale

A report about African animals and birds

A write-up of a science experiment

Section 9 — Paragraphs and Layout

2 Write a <u>subheading</u> for the first paragraph shown below.
Write your <u>own paragraph</u> for the second subheading.

Subheading 1: ....

There are many reasons why people have pets. Some people feel lonely without an animal friend to talk to. Many parents think that having an animal to care for teaches children to be responsible and kind. Some people just love animals!

Looking After Your Pet

....
....
....
....

3 Write a third paragraph about <u>pets</u>. Choose what you want to write about and write an <u>appropriate subheading</u>.

Subheading 3: ....

....
....
....
....

"I know when to use subheadings, and can write paragraphs with subheadings."

End of Punctuation Quiz

1 Correct the missing capital letters in the following sentence.

A french player called antoine joined liverpool football club, but he had to learn english to understand the manager.

1 mark

2 Add full stops and commas to the passage below. Correct any missing capital letters.

In the dark forest a goblin prodded the contents of a cauldron he wore a leather waistcoat and trousers made from an old potato sack as he stirred the mixture it gave off a stench of rotten eggs.

1 mark

3 Add commas to the following sentences where they are needed.

At two o'clock Chris Jones Erica and Harvey will arrive.

Add the chopped tomatoes onion and garlic to the pan.

Recently I have begun to play board games with my sister.

2 marks

4 Put a 'C' in the box if the apostrophe has been used for contraction or 'P' if it shows possession.

I don't think it's ready yet. ☐   James's room is untidy. ☐

Is that your dad's car? ☐   The fox's tail was fluffy. ☐

The fly's wings shimmered. ☐   The taxi's late. ☐

1 mark

© CGP — not to be photocopied

5 **Rewrite these phrases using an apostrophe to show possession.**

the bikes of two boys ....

the shoes of Angus ....

the play of the children ....

1 mark

6 **Rewrite these sentences with the correct punctuation for direct speech.**

Are the cakes finished asked Isla hungrily

....

Please be careful Kamal sighed Mum or you'll spill your tea.

....

....

2 marks

7 **Change this sentence from reported speech to direct speech.**

Mrs Anders told us to wipe our shoes as her carpet was new.

....

1 mark

8 **Write two sentences which include the words 'its' and 'it's'.**

(its) ....

(it's) ....

1 mark

I scored ____ out of 10.

Section 10 — Prefixes

Prefix: 're'

The prefix 're-' means 'again' or 'back'.

Most words with the 're-' prefix do not need a hyphen. **redesign**

But words where the root word begins with 'e', or which risk confusing the reader, will need a **hyphen**. **re-examine**

re-sent — 'resent' without a hyphen is a verb meaning 'begrudge'.

1) Use the 're-' prefix to shorten the underlined phrases. Write the new sentences out below.

Let me <u>assure you once again</u>: there are no spiders in the bath!

....

I had to <u>move to another place</u> the broken tile.

....

The archaeologists decided to <u>enter again</u> the tomb.

....

We had to <u>cover again</u> the bird's cage when it squawked.

....

2) Explain how the meaning of the underlined word is changed by adding a hyphen.

I had to <u>repair</u> the socks when they came out of the tumble drier.

repair means ....

re-pair means ....

Prefix: 'auto'

The prefix 'auto-' means 'self' or 'by oneself'.

For most of the flight, the plane was flown by the autopilot.

An autopilot is a machine that makes the plane fly itself.

1 Complete the sentences using the words in the box.

> autobiography   automatic   autograph
> automobile   autocue

There was an .... beep from the dishwasher when it finished its cycle.

The actor read her lines from an ....

Parked next to the kerb was a large American ....

The footballer's .... started when he was five.

The .... in the cover proved the diary was genuine.

2 Use a dictionary to find another word that starts with 'auto-'. Write down the word and its definition, then write it in a sentence.

auto ....

....

....

....

Negative Prefixes: 'il', 'im', 'in' and 'ir'

There are several prefixes beginning with 'i-' which change a word to its opposite meaning.

il- in- im- ir-

The prefix you use depends on the first letter of the root word.

correct → in<u>c</u>orrect

<u>p</u>ossible → im<u>p</u>ossible

1 Make a word with the opposite meaning to each word below by adding a negative prefix. Write it into the correct column of the table.

relevant   mortal   patient   legal
regular   logical   legible   polite
accurate   expensive   mobile   finite
responsible   considerate   balance

Try saying these words with the different prefixes. Which one sounds best? Use a dictionary to check the ones you aren't sure of.

il-	im-	in-	ir-

Section 10 — Prefixes

2 Use some of the words you created in Question 1 to complete these sentences.

It was .... to balance the antique vase on a wobbly pile of books.

Some people believe that there are an .... number of stars in the universe.

The game was ...., but the postage was very costly.

A smear of strawberry jam across the page had made the letter ....

Unfortunately, my clock was .... and I ended up being fifteen minutes late for the appointment.

Dad became .... with the man counting out his change at the checkout.

3 Use the table you created in Question 1 to complete these statements.

The prefix 'il-' is added to words that begin with the letter ....

An example of this is ....

The prefix 'im-' is added to words that begin with the letters .... , ... and .... An example of this is ....

The prefix 'ir-' is added to words that begin with the letter ....

An example of this is ....

Section 10 — Prefixes

Prefixes: 'anti' and 'multi'

The prefix 'anti-' means 'opposite' or 'against'.

anticlockwise ← This is the opposite direction to the one moved by the hands of a clock.

The prefix 'multi-' means 'many'.

multivitamin ← This means containing many vitamins.

1 Add 'anti-' or 'multi-' to the root words below.

...............social   ....septic   ....national

...............lingual   ....freeze   ....coloured

2 Complete the sentences below with words from Question 1.

Jane worked for a huge .... company.

The vet used .... to prevent infection.

Go away! I'm feeling ....

The explosion at the paint factory left the walls ....

3 Use a dictionary to find two other words which start with 'anti-' and 'multi-'. Write down the words and their definitions below.

anti........................... ....

....

multi........................... ....

....

Section 11 — Word Endings and Suffixes

Suffixes: 'ous'

The suffix '-ous' is used to form adjectives.

fame ⟶ famous

religion ⟶ religious

vary ⟶ various

Often you will have to **tweak** the letters at the **end** of the word when you **add the suffix**.

Words ending '-our' tend to drop the '-u-'.   humour ⟶ humorous

Words ending '-er' often drop the '-e-'.   monster ⟶ monstrous

1) Turn the words into **adjectives** by adding '**-ous**'. You may need to tweak the spellings. Use a dictionary to help you.

glamour ....   disaster ....

ambition ....   marvel ....

courage ....   suspicion ....

2) The **underlined** words have not been spelled correctly. Write out the passage with all words **correctly spelled**.

We walked <u>anx-uss-ly</u> down the <u>peril-uss</u> path. There were <u>poison-uss</u> toadstools along the path, and a <u>myster-uss</u> light shone from the abbey.

....
....
....
....

Suffixes: 'shun' / 'zhun' endings

Many verbs can be changed to nouns that have an ending which sounds like 'shun' or 'zhun'. You can spell it in several different ways.

When a word ends in '-t' or '-te', the ending is '-tion':

invent ➡ invention

If a word ends '-ss' or '-mit', the ending is '-ssion':

permit ➡ permission

If a word ends in a '-d', '-de' or '-se', it ends in '-sion':

invade ➡ invasion

Some nouns ending in '-c' or '-cs' change to a new noun by adding '-cian':

music ➡ musician

1 Give the words below a 'shun' or 'zhun' ending, and write them in the correct column of the table.

react   decide   possess   politics   confuse
transmit   magic   extend   mathematics   explode
direct   collect   demonstrate   optics   electric
logic   complete   persuade   confess   express

Use a dictionary to check the ones you aren't sure of.

-tion	-sion	-ssion	-cian

2 Read the <u>descriptions</u> of people's jobs below and write out the '-<u>cian</u>' word for each job.

I play instruments, sometimes more than one: ....

I fix your lights and your cooker if they break: ....

I solve complicated problems using numbers: ....

I do card tricks. I produce rabbits from hats: ....

You visit me yearly to get your eyes tested: ....

I sit in Parliament and help to run the country: ....

I deal with your IT at school. I fix computers: ....

3 Add an '-<u>sion</u>', '-<u>tion</u>', or '-<u>ssion</u>' to change the words in <u>brackets</u> so that they fit into the sentences below.

The price of (admit) .... to the zoo has gone up.

I can do multiplication, but (divide) .... defeats me!

We have an alarm for (protect) .... against burglars.

It is not wise to jump to (conclude) ....s .

4 Choose <u>three</u> other '-<u>shun</u>' words from Question 1. For each word you have chosen, write a <u>sentence</u> that uses it.

1. ....
2. ....
3. ....

Suffixes: Syllables and Doubling Consonants

Words have 'beats' you can clap. The beats are called 'syllables'.

1 syllable: fun, weigh, throne
2 syllables: saying, intend, butter
3 syllables: ungrateful, introduce, positive

A stressed syllable is one that your voice puts more weight on when you say the word. The underlined syllables here are the stressed syllables.

I re<u>cord</u> a song.

I make a <u>rec</u>ord of it.

1) Split the words into syllables. The first one has been done for you.

colourful co — lour — ful   admiration ....

feather ....   animal ....

mathematical ....

2) Underline the stressed syllable in each word below. The first two are done for you.

<u>but</u>ton   re<u>ply</u>   promise   over
enter   neglect   remain   children

3) The four words below have a different meaning depending on where the underlined stressed syllable is. Write a sentence using each one.

<u>sus</u>pect: ....

sus<u>pect</u>: ....

<u>pres</u>ent: ....

pre<u>sent</u>: ....

Section 11 — Word Endings and Suffixes

Sometimes you have to **double the consonant** at the end of a word when you **add certain suffixes**. This happens when the **last syllable** of the word is **stressed**.

for**ge**t + -ing → forge**tt**ing   **li**mit + -ing → lim**i**ting

The **last syllable is stressed**... ...so **the consonant ('t') is doubled**.   The **last syllable is not stressed**... ...so you **do not double the consonant**.

4) For each word below, put a tick in the box if the <u>last syllable</u> is <u>stressed</u> or a cross if it is not stressed. Choose a <u>suffix</u> to add, and write the new word.

word	stressed last syllable?		suffix ('-<u>ed</u>', '-<u>ing</u>' or '-<u>er</u>')		new word
prefer	✓	+	-ed	=	preferred
garden		+	....	=	....
occur		+	....	=	....
begin		+	....	=	....
visit		+	....	=	....

5) Choose <u>two words</u> from Question 4. Write each one in a sentence.

1. ....

2. ....

Word Endings: 'ture', 'sure', 'gue' and 'que'

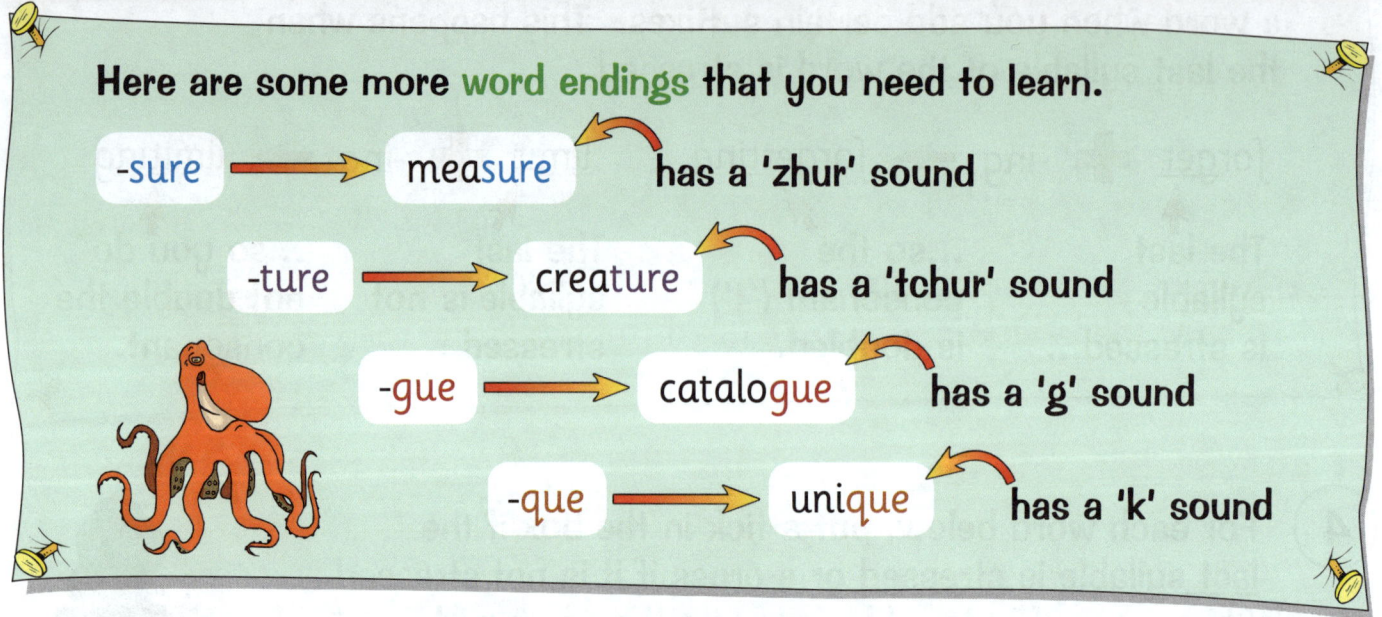

Here are some more word endings that you need to learn.

- -sure → measure has a 'zhur' sound
- -ture → creature has a 'tchur' sound
- -gue → catalogue has a 'g' sound
- -que → unique has a 'k' sound

1 Spell the words below correctly. They should all end with either '-sure', '-ture', '-gue' or '-que'.

pleazhur .... anteek ....

mixtchur .... colleag ....

leag .... leizhur ....

adventchur .... dialog ....

2 Add the correct word endings to complete the sentences below.

The Black Death was a terrible pla.................. .

You'll get pla.................. if you don't clean your teeth twice a day.

The x-ray showed that my arm had a frac.................. .

You'll have to mea.................. to see if it will fit.

I don't know exactly, but I have a va.................. idea.

The teacher showed great displea.................. when I failed my test.

Section 11 — Word Endings and Suffixes © CGP — not to be photocopied

Section 12 — Confusing Words

Words Containing 'sc' Making An 's' Sound

Sometimes 'sc' is used to make an 's' sound.

scene   **mu sc le**

Most of these words come from Latin. There is no easy way to spot these words, so you'll need to learn them.

1) Add **letters** into the boxes so that the words **match** their **definitions**.

Very interesting	f		s	c					
To go down			s	c			
A teenager	a	d			s	c		
The features of a landscape			s	c				y
Controlled behaviour	d		s	c		p			

2) Rearrange the letters in the **boxes** to create an '**sc**' word, then draw lines to match each word to the **correct definition**.

n i c e c
s .... e

e n c
s .... t

e c n s
a .... d

i s o r c s
s .... s

- Climb or rise up
- Physics, chemistry or biology
- A tool for cutting things
- Smell or odour

Tricky Homophones

Homophones are words that have a different spelling and meaning, but which sound the same. You will need to learn which is the correct meaning for each word to avoid mistakes like this.

Adam used his queue to knock in the snooker ball. ✗

Adam used his cue to knock in the snooker ball. ✓

1 Circle the incorrect homophones in each sentence, then write out the sentence correctly.

The material was course and made his skin saw.

....

The loan night road out to battle.

....

The protester drew a piece cymbal on the wall.

....

Their was nothing to do on the plain but stair out of the window.

....

....

2 A pair of homophones can be written in the gaps below to complete the sentences. Work out which pair of homophones to use and write the correct word in each gap.

The .... was moved into the palace.

When the window broke, we all looked at

the girl who had .... the ball.

Section 12 — Confusing Words

3 Using the incorrect homophone can create a strange image in the reader's mind. For each sentence, draw a picture in the box to show the images created by using the incorrect homophone.

I found the baked beans in a supermarket isle. →

The waiter brought a strawberry moose for dessert. →

We saw a lot of fowls during the football match. →

Unstressed and Silent Vowels

Unstressed vowels are vowel sounds that you can't hear clearly.

poison *sounds like* poisun

Sometimes they sound like a **different vowel**.

boundary *sounds like* boundry

Sometimes they sound like they're **not there at all**.

1 The words in the box have <u>unstressed vowels</u>. Write each word in the <u>correct column</u> of the table and <u>underline</u> the unstressed vowel.

~~generous~~   ~~dictionary~~   stationary   difference
chocolate   history   parliament   general
interesting   factory   business   calendar

unstressed <u>a</u>	unstressed <u>e</u>	unstressed <u>i</u>	unstressed <u>o</u>
diction<u>a</u>ry	gen<u>e</u>rous		

2 Fill in all the <u>missing vowels</u> in the words below. Use a dictionary to check them if you need to.

.... b .... nd .... n .... d   d .... f .... n .... t .... ly

s .... p .... r .... t .... r .... g .... n .... lly

Words from the Year 3/4 Spelling List

Below are all the words on the Year 3 and 4 spelling list. By the end of Year 4, you should be able to spell these words correctly.

The following pages will help you learn the most challenging of these words.

1) Put a tick, cross or question mark next to each word to show how confident you are with the spelling of the word.

accident(ally)	disappear	interest	pressure
actual(ly)	early	island	probably
address	earth	knowledge	promise
answer	eight/eighth	learn	purpose
appear	enough	length	quarter
arrive	exercise	library	question
believe	experience	material	recent
bicycle	experiment	medicine	regular
breath	extreme	mention	reign
breathe	famous	minute	remember
build	favourite	natural	sentence
busy/business	February	naughty	separate
calendar	forward(s)	notice	special
caught	fruit	occasion(ally)	straight
centre	grammar	often	strange
century	group	opposite	strength
certain	guard	ordinary	suppose
circle	guide	particular	surprise
complete	heard	peculiar	therefore
consider	heart	perhaps	though/although
continue	height	popular	thought
decide	history	position	through
describe	imagine	possess(ion)	various
different	increase	possible	weight
difficult	important	potatoes	woman/women

Section 12 — Confusing Words

2 Circle the correct spelling in each pair of words below.

- accidently / **accidentally**
- bisiness / **business**
- **disappear** / disapear
- actualy / **actually**
- **different** / diffrent
- naurty / **naughty**
- **grammar** / grammer
- wieght / **weight**

3 Complete the sentences using the correct spellings from Question 2.

The children .... spilt water on the carpet.

"I have made your doughnut .... ," said Tim, brushing sugar from his mouth.

It's .... to run in school — except in an emergency.

What's in my diary is none of your ....

4 Cross out and correct any incorrectly spelled words below.

She found it hard to ~~breath~~, but she still had some strenth left.
.... breathe ....

The king promised to his people that his rain would be peaceful.
....

The doctor said he should continue to take the medecine for his high blood presure.
....

Section 12 — Confusing Words

Identifying **smaller words** within your spellings can be a helpful strategy. For example, the words 'know' and 'ledge' are in the word 'knowledge'.

know + ledge = knowledge

5 Underline any smaller words that occur <u>within the words</u> below. Then <u>cover</u> each word and write it out on the line underneath.

favourite
....

heard
....

peculiar
....

quarter
....

6 The words below have been spelled incorrectly. Write the <u>correct spelling</u> for each word.

libary .... suprise ....

exersise .... intrest ....

hieght .... particuler ....

ordinery .... ocasional ....

experiance .... centry ....

sentance .... reguler ....

Section 12 — Confusing Words

End of Spelling Quiz

1 Circle the **correct spelling** for the **underlined words** in each sentence.

The teacher had to <u>remark</u> / <u>re-mark</u> the test.

I <u>resent</u> / <u>re-sent</u> having to send a thank-you card.

1 mark

2 Write words that start with the prefix '<u>in</u>', '<u>im</u>', '<u>il</u>' or '<u>ir</u>' to <u>match each definition</u>.

against the law	cannot be done
i .... g l	i .... ss .... b .... e

not on the subject	childish
i .... lev .... t	i .... t .... r ....

1 mark

3 Change these words into **adjectives**.

courage ➡ ....   continue ➡ ....

religion ➡ ....   fame ➡ ....

fury ➡ ....   anxiety ➡ ....

1 mark

4 Rewrite each word with an <u>ending</u> that has the <u>shun/zhun sound</u>. You may also need to <u>remove some letters</u>.

decide ....   magic ....

collide ....   explode ....

compete ....   admit ....

music ....   suspect ....

2 marks

5 Underline the correct spelling in each pair.

prefered / preferred

begining / beginning

gardener / gardenner

labeled / labelled

limited / limitted

traveled / travelled

happening / happenning

preferable / preferrable

1 mark

6 Write the correct spelling to match each clue.

ack-see-dent ....

sur-tun ....

o-kay-shun-ally ....

nor-tee ....

op-o-set ....

se-pur-ut ....

2 marks

7 Rearrange the letters to make words ending in 'gue' or 'que'.

eaglue ....

quineu ....

squome ....

gufatie ....

1 mark

8 Cross out any incorrect spellings below and write the correct spellings above.

Pippa left the supermarket isle and stood in the cue.

The cymbal on the rode sign showed there was no way threw.

My dog will stair at a peace of cake until he is given sum.

1 mark

I scored ☐ out of 10.

End of Book Test

1 **Tick the sentence that is <u>correctly punctuated</u>.**

"Leave the door open, said Kim, while I go outside." ☐

"Leave the door open," said Kim, "while I go outside". ☐

"Leave the door open," said Kim, "while I go outside." ☐

"Leave the door open" said Kim, "while I go outside". ☐

1 mark

2 **Choose <u>pronouns</u> from the boxes to complete the sentences.**

.... visit the same beach every summer. .... doesn't get too busy and there's a lovely café there.

She   We   The beach   It

1 mark

3 **Underline the <u>adverbial</u> that says <u>where</u> the egg and spoon race will happen. Add a <u>fronted adverbial</u> to show <u>when</u> it will happen.**

...., the egg and spoon race will take place on the other side of the football pitch.

1 mark

4 **Underline the <u>subordinate clause</u> in the sentence and add an <u>expanded noun phrase</u> to describe what Daisy bought her mother.**

Because it was her mother's birthday, Daisy bought her

....

....

1 mark

5 Circle the determiner and underline the possessive pronouns in the sentence below.

Charlie took some pens, but they were mine, not his.

1 mark

6 Find all the examples of simple past, past progressive and present perfect verb forms in the passage below.

   Jess charged up the pitch. She wasn't looking where she was going and bumped into Aaliyah.
   "Ouch!" she yelled, "Why were you in the way? I've hurt my ankle now!"

simple past: ....

past progressive: ....

present perfect: ....

1 mark

7 Join the three sentences below to make one sentence. Use conjunctions and make at least one clause a subordinate clause.

Ben made a cake. It was Ethan's birthday. He burnt it.

....

....

1 mark

8 Rewrite the sentence below so that the tenses are correct.

Before he arrived, we are locked in the house.

....

1 mark

© CGP — not to be photocopied

9 Add the prefix beginning with 'i' that turns the word into its opposite.

..........possible   ....responsible   ....secure

..........legal   ....mortal   ....credible

1 mark

10 Circle the word that contains an apostrophe that shows possession.

If they're sure their TV won't work, we'll have to watch the film at Noah's.

1 mark

11 Add the correct 'shun' ending ('tion', 'sion' or 'cian') to each word.

ten..................	electri..................	men..................
elec.................	man....................	mis..................
po...................	musi...................	confu................

1 mark

12 Rewrite these sentences with the correct punctuation.

without looking he stepped out into the road

....

with an evil chuckle harriet closed the lid

....

i cant go on tuesday ive got to go to liverpool.

....

1 mark

13 Rewrite the passage correctly so that <u>singular verbs</u> agree with <u>singular nouns</u> and <u>plural verbs</u> agree with <u>plural nouns</u>.

Planting seeds are fun. Each type of seed develop in a different number of days. When the young plants has four leaves, you can put them in bigger pots.

....

....

....

1 mark

14 Underline the <u>expanded noun phrase</u> in the sentence below.

Rover chased a squirrel up the tallest oak tree in the park while barking enthusiastically.

1 mark

15 Circle the <u>abstract nouns</u> in the list below.

happiness	Thursday	tension	cash
French	hope	tray	animal
furniture	crowd	stupidity	luck

1 mark

16 Rewrite the sentences below so that the <u>correct personal pronouns</u> are used.

Mum gave Dan and I a choice of rewards.

....

Bobby and me asked if we could go out.

....

1 mark

© CGP — not to be photocopied

17 Complete the sentence below with an **adverbial of cause**.

He took a book with him ....

....

18 Complete the sentences using the **words in the boxes**.

[singer's]   [singers']   [child's]   [children's]

The .... playground was full of noise.

I listened to the .... solo.

We returned the .... toy to her mother.

The conductor checked the .... costumes.

19 Circle the **correct spellings**.

accidently   surprise   calander   suprise

occasion   calendar   accidentally   occassion

20 Choose a word to write in the gap below. Write the **word class** of the word you've added in the box.

Everybody was jealous of Tina's .... pencil case.

word class: ....

21 Underline the **two adverbs** in the sentence below.

Isla's new puppy chased its tail happily and almost knocked over the table.

22 Underline the main clause in this sentence.

When swans are disturbed, they can become violent.

1 mark

23 Draw a double line (//) to show where there should be a paragraph break in the passage below.

All night I tossed and turned as worry upon worry filled my thoughts. It felt like I would never sleep and the clock on my bedside table reminded me of how soon I would have to go back to school. In the morning, the world seemed strangely quiet and when I pulled back my curtains, I couldn't believe my eyes. My garden and the road beyond it was covered by a deep layer of snow!

1 mark

24 Rewrite these sentences into Standard English.

I should of seen the doctor earlier.

....

Tim and me wasn't sure which was the bestest way to go.

....

1 mark

25 Rewrite the direct speech below with the correct punctuation.

My car won't start said Amy and the garage is closed.

....

1 mark

I scored [ ] out of 25.

Glossary

Adjective — A word that describes a noun, e.g. **spicy** curry.

Adverb — A word that describes a verb, e.g. end **abruptly**.

Adverbial — A word, phrase or clause that behaves like an **adverb**.

Clause — Part of a sentence that contains a **subject** (**someone** or **something** doing the action) and a **verb**.

Command — A sentence that gives an **instruction** or an **order**.

Conjunction — A word or phrase that **joins** two parts of a sentence.

Determiner — Tells you if a **noun** is **general** or **specific**.
e.g. I would like <u>a</u> drink. I would like <u>that</u> drink.

Direct speech — The **actual words** the speaker says.

Exclamation — A sentence that shows **strong feelings**, beginning with 'how' or 'what'.

Heading — A description of the **main topic** of the text.

Main clause — A clause that **makes sense** on its own.
e.g. <u>I like football</u> because it is fun.

Noun — A word that **names** something, e.g. **cat**, **James**, **Monday**.

Paragraph — Used to **group** related sentences **together**.

Phrase — A group of words usually without a **verb**.

Preposition — Tells you **where**, **when** or **why** something happens.

Reported speech — A **description** of someone's speech.

Glossary

Statement — A sentence that **tells** you something.

Subordinate clause — A clause that **doesn't make sense** on its own, e.g. I like football <u>because it is fun</u>.

Verb — A doing or being word, e.g. **run**, **appear**, **shout**, **be**.

COMMON PUNCTUATION MARKS

Apostrophes — show **missing letters** and **possession**.	'
Capital letters — used for **starting** sentences, **proper nouns** and **I**.	A
Commas — used in **lists**, to separate **extra information** and after **fronted adverbials**.	,
Exclamation marks — show **exclamations**, **commands** or **strong emotions**.	!
Full stops — show where **sentences end**.	.
Inverted commas — show **direct speech**.	" "
Question marks — used at the **end** of **questions**.	?

VERB FORMS

Past Progressive — I **was doing**, you **were doing**, etc.

Present Progressive — I **am doing**, you **are doing**, etc.

Present Perfect — I **have done**, you **have done**, etc.

Answers

Grammar

Section 1 — Word Classes

Pages 4 and 5 — Different Types of Noun

1. Proper Nouns: **Okavango River, Africa, Lake Ngami, Botswana**
   Common Nouns — Concrete: **wolves, robin, elephant, spade, metal, bottle**
   Common Nouns — Abstract: **freedom, courage, hunger, joy, beauty, peace**
   Common Nouns — Collective: **fleet, herd, tribe, flock**

2. **Thirst** is the feeling of needing a drink. — Abstract
   Rain is water that falls from clouds. — Concrete
   A **crowd** is a large gathering of people. — Collective

3. There are lots of possible answers to this question.
   Examples:
   I take **pride** in my work.
   Happiness is the most important thing.

4. There are lots of possible answers to this question.
   Example:
   We travelled to Ireland. We saw a flock of sheep in the mountains. To our amazement, there were also some lambs.

Pages 6 and 7 — Adjectives: Comparative and Superlative

1. Comparative: **more lovely, darker, more graceful, less pleasant, prettier**
   Superlative: **least helpful, hottest, strongest, most dangerous, sunniest, smallest, most courageous**.

2. There are lots of possible answers to this question.
   Examples:
   My brother is **shorter** than me.
   Today is the **coldest** day of the year.

3. **happy** — happier — **happiest**
   annoying — **more annoying** — most annoying
   expensive — less expensive — least expensive
   easy — **easier** — easiest
   bright — brighter — **brightest**
   bad — **worse** — **worst**
   good — **better** — best

4. Jeri is **taller** than I am, but Meg is the **tallest**.
   This book is **more expensive / less expensive** than that one.
   Mum's quite fussy but Dad is even **fussier**.
   Out of all of us, Josh is the **cleverest**.
   York is the **most interesting** city I've visited.
   You need a **sharper** knife than the one you have.

5. Any suitable explanation.
   Example:
   Comparatives are used for comparing one thing with another. Superlatives are used for saying which thing is the most or least.

Pages 8 and 9 — Using Adverbs

1. You should have circled:
   funny (adjective)
   played (verb)
   simple (adjective)

2. There are lots of possible answers to this question.
   Examples:
   It was a **terribly** dark night.
   Shaun had been acting **strangely** all day.
   If you speak that **fast**, no one will understand.
   It's **quite** surprising that he arrived so **early**.

3. There are lots of possible answers to this question.
   Examples:
   My house has a **really** beautiful garden.
   She felt **somewhat** sick after eating all that chocolate.
   The beach was **pretty** clean, and there was no litter.
   She is having a **fairly** difficult time at the moment.
   The weather was **much** worse today than yesterday.
   Climbing that tree was a **hugely** dangerous thing to do.

4. There are lots of possible answers to this question.
   Examples:
   She was **especially** talented.
   It was **quite** loud.

Page 10 — Personal and Possessive Pronouns

1. Any suitable personal or possessive pronouns.
   Examples:
   "That cake is **yours** and this cake is **mine**," she said.
   Ella said **she** would read my story if I read **hers**.
   "This hedge of **yours** is too high," Joe said. "I need a ladder."
   The dogs thought the food was **theirs**, so **they** ate it!
   Ned and I said the ball was **ours** and **we** wanted it back.

Answers

2. There are lots of possible answers to this question. Example:
   I told **him** that the book was **mine**. **He** disagreed and said the book was actually **his**.

3. It is unclear if it is Laura, her friend or someone else that can't go to the party.

Page 11 — Determiners

1. Different answers are possible for this question. Example:
   I tried to pick **an** apple from **the** highest branch but I fell to **the** ground. I ripped **a** hole in my jeans but **these** jeans are old. **Some** apples on the tree were fine, but **one** apple had maggots in it.

2. Fussy Phil: **those pens, the Daily Blurb, Arthur's cakes, three apples**
   Easy Ernie: **some pencils, many biscuits, a newspaper, a few doughnuts, lots of pears**

Section 2 — Verb Forms

Pages 12 and 13 — Using Past Tense Verb Forms

1. she has answered — present perfect
   you were thinking — past progressive
   he was building — past progressive
   they remembered — simple past
   I have caught — present perfect
   we promised — simple past
   we were deciding — past progressive
   he has noticed — present perfect
   I was guarding — past progressive
   you mentioned — simple past
   they have learned — present perfect
   she imagined — simple past

2. There are lots of possible answers to this question. Examples:
   simple past: They went to London at the weekend.
   past progressive: I was playing tennis with Sofia.
   present perfect: We have baked a cake today.

3. There are lots of possible answers to this question. Examples:
   We were watching TV before you saw us.
   I was running when he grabbed me.

4. There's more than one possible answer for some of the answers to this question. Example:
   'I'm going out,' **said** Dad. 'I **have made** you a salad for lunch. Enjoy!'
   After lunch, we **tidied** and **cleaned** the kitchen. I **was thinking** about building my model plane, but Jaz **wanted** to go out in the garden. We **were arguing** about it, when there **was** a knock on the door. The postman **was standing** there with a package.
   'I nearly **broke** my back carrying this,' he **puffed**.
   The number of times you've used each past tense form depends on which words you've used. In this example, simple past: 7, past progressive: 3, present perfect: 1.

Pages 14 and 15 — Using Different Tenses

1. Here is a sensible order for the sentences. Starting from the first sentence:
   7, 3 (or 4), 1, 6, 2, 4 (or 3), 5

2. Yesterday, I ~~go~~ **went** to karate after school. I ~~enjoy~~ **enjoyed** it, but my friend Sam ~~was hating~~ **hated** it and said it ~~is~~ **was** boring. We walked home together and I ~~carry~~ **carried** his bag because ~~he's~~ **he was** really tired.

3. There are lots of possible answers to this question.

Section 3 — Phrases and Clauses

Page 16 — Expanded Noun Phrases

1. 10 Downing Street — the official home of the Prime Minister of the United Kingdom
   Irish Sea — a body of water separating Britain and Ireland
   Loch Ness — Any suitable description.
   For example: a lake in Scotland said to contain a monster
   Pennines — a range of hills sometimes called the 'backbone of England'

2. Example:
   Mars — red planet fourth closest to the Sun

Page 17 — Main and Subordinate Clauses

1. (I can help you) if you'd like me to.
   After it had stopped raining, I went outside for a stroll.
   (Suki really likes cycling) but (she can't stand jogging)
   Although they loved travelling, (they decided to stay at home) until Bill was in better health.

Answers

2. There are lots of possible answers to this question. Example:
   Hayley was late because there were no buses running, so Larry had to wait for her.

Pages 18 and 19 — Adverbials

1. before school — adverbial
   Jack came in — main clause
   outside the door — adverbial
   we pretended to read — main clause
   with a huge crash — adverbial
   the phone rang — main clause
   because he missed her — adverbial
   suddenly — adverbial
   we got a surprise — main clause
   before she arrived — adverbial

2. The climber rested <u>for a few moments</u>. **phrase**
   I do ballet <u>at the church hall</u>. **phrase**
   <u>Although we were tired</u>, we couldn't stop. **subordinate clause**
   <u>Luckily</u>, I found a five pound note. **adverb**
   They fell asleep <u>after they'd eaten</u>. **subordinate clause**

3. There are lots of possible answers to this question. Examples:
   Yesterday, I had to go shopping.
   I had to go shopping **with my mum**.
   After I'd done my homework, I had to go shopping.

4. There are lots of possible answers to this question. Example:
   I knew that the dinosaur had not eaten <u>that day</u>, so I ran <u>as fast as I could</u>. <u>Ahead of me</u>, I could see a small cottage. <u>If I could reach the cottage</u>, I could hide <u>there</u>. <u>All of a sudden</u>, I heard a loud roar <u>behind me</u>. <u>The next moment</u>, I heard a huge crash and thud <u>as the dinosaur fell to the floor</u>.

5. There are lots of possible answers to this question. Example:
   An adverbial is an adverb, phrase or subordinate clause which tells you how, where, when or how often something happens.

Section 4 — Using Adverbials

Pages 20 and 21 — Adverbials of Time

1. Adverbials of time: As soon as the sun rose, then, The day before, later on, that night, This morning, when he opened the cupboard, After you'd gone to bed, since yesterday morning, tomorrow, NOW, every day, soon

2. There are lots of possible answers to this question. Examples:
   First, finally, after that, when we got there, before lunch, next.

3. Many different sentences are possible. Example:
   As soon as her alarm sounded, she jumped out of bed.
   When the cat hissed at the dog, it made him bark, and the cat ran away instantly.
   As we sailed into the harbour, the wind was rising. Suddenly, there was a loud crack. The mast broke, and all the sails fell onto the deck. For several seconds, we could not see anything, and moments later, we bumped into the harbour wall.

4. There are lots of possible answers to this question. Example:
   <u>As soon as we realised what had happened</u>, we rushed to see if there was any more damage to the ship.

Pages 22 and 23 — Adverbials of Place

1. There are lots of possible answers to this question. Examples:
   bear — **behind a rock**
   girls — **nearby**
   dwarf — **in front of the bear**
   town — **in the distance**

2. There are lots of possible answers to this question. Example:
   As the girls hid nearby, the bear jumped out from behind a rock.
   The dwarf waved his arms and sank to his knees in front of the bear.

Answers

3. There are lots of possible answers to this question. Examples:
   In the middle of the ocean, the lonely ship sailed onwards.
   The spy lurked silently **in the alleyway**.
   At the bottom of the garden, the fairy danced in the moonlight.
   The cheetah sprinted **towards its prey**.
   Outside the stadium, the fans started to gather.
   He sat quietly **in the waiting room**.

4. There are lots of possible answers to this question.

Pages 24 and 25 — Adverbials of Cause

1. The following adverbials should be underlined:
   Since it is written in French
   in case I fall off it
   As you are so keen
   due to problems with his car
   because she might run away

2. There are lots of possible answers to this question. Examples:
   I stayed at home **because I was too tired**.
   We ought to go shopping **before it gets dark**.
   Because of the bad weather, we will have to postpone our trip.
   Since it's nice and sunny, we should have a picnic.

3. There are lots of possible answers to this question.

4. There are lots of possible answers to this question. Example:
   They couldn't watch TV since Mum had hidden the remote. Therefore, Kie decided to teach the dog to walk on its hind legs. As the dog didn't enjoy this very much, he got cross and knocked over a table and broke a vase.

Page 26 — Adverbials in Fiction & Non-Fiction

1. There are lots of possible answers to this question. Make sure your answer includes adverbials of time, place and cause.

2. There are lots of possible answers to this question. Make sure your answer includes adverbials of time, place and cause.

Section 5 — Writing Style

Page 27 — Common Error 1: 'Have' or 'Of'

1. I might ~~of~~ **have** known.
   I'd never ~~of~~ **have** thought of that.
   ~~Have~~ **Of** course you should!
   They didn't go, but maybe they should ~~of~~ **have**.
   "You should've seen it!" he said, laughing. (This last sentence is fine as it is written speech.)

2. There are lots of possible answers to this question.

Page 28 — Common Error 2: Pronouns with 'and'

1. The following sentences should be ticked:
   David and I will do it.
   You can trust David and me.
   I think he and I should go.

2. Benji and **I** decided to sneak out. It was a bit naughty of my brother and **me**, but we risked it anyway. Rachael spotted us leaving but didn't say anything. **She** and **I** have always got on.

Page 29 — Common Error 3: Comparatives and Superlatives

1. **the funniest joke**
   'Funniest' already means the most funny.
   an inferior product
   'Inferior' already means lower in quality. It's already a comparative.
   the mountain's summit
   'Summit' already means the highest point.
   the ideal place
   'Ideal' already means 'most perfect'. It's already a superlative.

Pages 30 and 31 — Verb Agreement and Standard Verb Forms

1. There are several possible answers to this question. Here's one way of matching them up:
   A bear — catches the salmon.
   The elephants — eat sugar cane.
   My Nan — drinks tea.
   The athlete — runs marathons.
   Three sisters — meet at midnight.

Answers

2. The following words should be underlined: <u>freeze</u>, <u>become</u>, <u>does</u>, <u>sink</u>, <u>forms</u>, <u>turn</u>
   The rewritten passage should read:
   Water **freezes** at 0 °C and **becomes** ice. This frozen water floats on liquid water. Most other substances **do** not behave in this way; their frozen form **sinks** in the liquid form. When you heat water to 100 °C, bubbles **form** and water **turns** into a gas.

3. <u>We was</u> — We were
   <u>You seen</u> — You saw
   <u>I ain't</u> — I'm not
   <u>They been</u> — They went
   <u>She done</u> — She did
   <u>I've went</u> — I've gone

4. We ~~was~~ **were** on our way to the shops when we ~~seen~~ **saw** a horse galloping down the road. It had ~~ran~~ **run** away from its owner. I ~~begun~~ **began** to panic. Mum was fearless though and ran to catch it. We put a scarf round its neck to hold it and ~~given~~ **gave** it a carrot, but while we ~~was~~ **were** waiting for its owner, it ~~done~~ **did** a wee over Mum's shoes.

End of Grammar Quiz

Pages 32 and 33

1. Concrete: gate, carpet, oak
   Abstract: courage, fear, trust
   Proper: **M**onday, **L**ondon, **F**errari
   Collective: crowd, flock, tribe
   [2 marks for all 12 words in the correct boxes, or just 1 mark for a minimum of 6 words in the correct boxes] **Note: to get the marks for the proper nouns, the first letter must be a capital.**

2. Can you donate <u>any</u> clothes? — **determiner**
   Danny wants <u>me</u> to tie his laces — **pronoun**
   His cooking is <u>really</u> terrible. — **adverb**
   [1 mark]

3. Samir was running in an obstacle race. — past progressive
   Who has eaten my biscuit? — present perfect
   I saw your friend in town. — simple past
   They weren't helping us. — past progressive
   [1 mark]

4. Are these sunglasses ⟨yours⟩? I think I have lost ⟨mine⟩ *[1 mark]*

5. The jewels were stolen <u>before I could raise the alarm</u>.
   <u>Once the weather improved</u>, we went ahead with the barbecue and had a great time.
   [1 mark]

6. more happy — **happier**
   most strange — **strangest**
   most bad — **worst**
   most pretty — **prettiest**
   most boring — **most boring**
   more good — **better**
   [2 marks for all answers correct, or 1 mark if you got three, four or five answers correct]

7. <u>As it was raining</u>, the swimming pool was packed. — **cause**
   The tiny lizard lounged <u>on the side of the wall</u>. — **place**
   [1 mark]

8. Dad built a slide in the garden for my sister and **me**.
   Izzy and **I** solved the puzzle together.
   My brother and **I** made a terrible mess.
   [1 mark]

Answers

Punctuation

Section 6 — Sentence Punctuation

Pages 34 and 35 — Capital Letters

1. **O**n **V**alentine's **D**ay, I received a card addressed to **M**r **S**nuffles.
   The book **D**ad read was about the **R**oyal **A**ir **F**orce.
   In the spring of 1774, the **B**ritish explorer **J**ames **C**ook arrived at **E**aster **I**sland in the **P**acific **O**cean.

2. Scotland – **Scottish**
   Italy – **Italian**
   Denmark – **Danish**
   Elizabeth – **Elizabethan**
   Rome – **Roman**
   Canada – **Canadian**
   Shakespeare – Shakespearean
   Victoria – Victorian
   Mars – Martian
   Israel – Israeli
   For example:
   America – American
   Cornwall – Cornish

3. Any suitable answer, for example:
   Stan Laurel was an actor who came from the **Cumbrian** town of Ulverston.

Pages 36 and 37 — Punctuation for the End of a Sentence

1. **Questions** should always end with a question mark.
   You use **commands** when you're telling someone what to do. These can end with a full stop or an exclamation mark, depending on how forceful or urgent they are.
   Exclamations are sentences like, "What a nice day it is!"
   Statements should end with a full stop, unless they show a lot of emotion, in which case they can end with an exclamation mark.

2. I have two sisters**.**
   What a pain you are**!**
   What did he say**?**
   Look out**!**
   Pass the sugar please, Milly**.**
   I asked him a question**.**
   Could you help me, please**?**
   It was so amazing**!**

3. **I**'m so jealous**.** (or **I**'m so jealous**!**) **W**hat an amazing holiday**!** **I**'ve never been to **A**merica**.** **D**id you go by plane**?** **W**here did you stay**?**

4. Any suitable answers.
   Examples:
   We use punctuation marks to help us to understand the meaning of a sentence.
   We use 3 different punctuation marks to help us tell the reader what type of sentence they're reading. For example, if a sentence ends with a question mark, they know that someone is asking a question.

Section 7 — Commas and Apostrophes

Page 38 — Commas or Full Stops?

1. Before we had dinner**,** we played in the park.
   It was 8 o'clock by the time we ate.
   As the spectators applauded**,** Gary struggled to reach the bench. **T**hat last tackle had really hurt him.

2. **I**t was the day of the athletics competition. **E**ach day after she had finished school**,** Milly had practised on the field near her house. **N**ow she was ready. **B**efore she left**,** she checked her bag one more time. **E**verything was there**.**

Page 39 — Commas for Lists

1. Any suitable answers.
   Examples:
   The greengrocer's colourful display included a yellow lemon, **two green watermelons, six red apples, three pots of blueberries and a punnet of peaches.**
   At the alphabetical party, there was an artist from Albania, **a builder from Belgium, a cyclist from Cyprus, a dentist from Denmark and an elephant from Ethiopia.**

2. Any suitable answers.
   Examples:
   Please buy the following four items: **chocolate biscuits, ice cream, fruit and juice.**
   Please buy the following five items: **chocolate, biscuits, ice cream, fruit and juice.**

Page 40 — Commas with Fronted Adverbials

1. In the cupboard**,** a family of mice feasted on biscuit crumbs.
   With an angry yell**,** my sister snatched back her lollipop.
   Before the film had started**,** the boys had eaten all their popcorn.

Answers

2. **With a mighty shot,** Sophia scored the winning goal.
   Whenever I give her parsley, my guinea pig squeals.

Page 41 — Apostrophes for Contraction

1. weren't
   they're
   doesn't
   haven't

2. Who had
   They would
   Nobody has
   There is

3. There are lots of possible answers to this question. Make sure yours includes at least two contractions.
   Example:
   It's not my fault you're clumsy.

Pages 42 and 43 — Apostrophes for Plural Possession

1. The elephants' tusks
   The animals' tracks
   The bees' hive

2. The cars' lights — The lights of more than one car
   Fergus's school — The school of one boy called Fergus
   The foxes' den — The den of more than one fox
   The fly's wings — The wings of one fly
   The bus's seats — The seats of one bus

3. men's ties
   sheep's wool
   team's field
   girls' bikes
   mice's food
   wolves' howls

4. Any suitable answers.
   Examples:
   Marcus's property
   The trees' leaves
   The cats' mouse
   The babies' cot

Page 44 — Its / It's and Whose / Who's

1. We found a cat. I don't know **its** name but **it's** probably from the house on the corner.
   If **it's** too late to go swimming, can you get out my bike and pump up **its** tyres?
   The car failed **its** test and now **it's** being scrapped.

2. I think I know **whose** shoes are in the bush, but I don't know **who's** responsible for putting them there.
   "**Who's** been to Paris?" asked the teacher.
   "**Who's** going there this summer?"
   I don't know **whose** story to believe.

Section 8 — Punctuation for Speech

Page 45 — Moving the Reporting Clause

1. "I do like Mrs Oxley**,**" he said**,** "but she can be a bit fierce."

2. There are lots of possible answers to this question. Make sure yours includes a piece of speech with the reporting clause in the middle.
   Example:
   "We're nearly there now," I said, "so you can stop complaining."

Pages 46 and 47 — Adding Information to the Reporting Clause

1. Any suitable answers.
   Examples:
   "Stop it," said Hanna **angrily**. "It's not fair to tease."
   "Do I have to go to school?" Andy enquired **daily**.
   "I'd quite like to go home," said Jill **wearily**. "I'm tired."
   "OK, what can I do for you?" asked Shruti **cheerfully**.
   John muttered **softly**, "I've had enough of this."
   "What a mess!" Mum exclaimed **furiously**. "Clear it up!"
   Jin said **sadly**, "I wonder if it'll ever look clean."

2. There are lots of possible answers to this question. Make sure yours include reporting clauses which add extra information to each line of speech.
   Examples:
   "Wherever we go," **cried Lola softly, wiping the tears from her eyes,** "I think we will always be the best of friends."
   "There are old mines from the war on this beach," **shouted the tour guide loudly, taking care to watch where he put his feet.** "Be careful!"
   "I've always liked adventure," **explained the explorer proudly to the journalist,** "but of course not everyone does."

3. "Can we go straight down to the beach**?**" asked Tash**,** dumping her bag on the bed**.** "I really want to go swimming**.**"

Answers

Pages 48 and 49 — Reported and Direct Speech

1. You should have matched these pairs:
   She told me she was cold. — "I'm cold," she cried.
   "Come here, please," I said. — I told her to come over to me.
   "What a nuisance!" she said. — She exclaimed that it was a nuisance.
   She said she was too tired to go. — "I'm too tired to go," she said.
   I asked if her dog was very old. — "Is your dog very old?" I said.
   He said that he didn't like milk. — "I don't like milk," he said.
   Mum told me to put my stuff away. — "Put your stuff away!" said Mum.

2. There are lots of possible answers to this question.
   Examples:
   "I much prefer playing rugby to football," said Raj.
   "I can't (or 'couldn't') do that maths work," Megan replied.

3. "I don't mind walking, but I'd prefer to get the bus," said Mary to Nenad.
   "There aren't any buses going to the beach," explained Nenad.
   "I hope there's an ice cream van there," said Mary, "because I want a choc ice."

Section 9 — Paragraphs and Layout

Pages 50 and 51 — Using Paragraphs

1. You should have added these paragraph markers:
   "Where did he go?" gasped Josh, stopping suddenly. "I can't see which street he went down!" **// (new person speaking)** "I'm not sure," Ellie said, just as exhausted as Josh. "I think we're going to have to split up. You grab his collar, and I'll take his lead. At least that way we'll each have something to hold him with." **// (change of time)** It had seemed like an easy thing to do at first, offering to dog-sit Mr Knight's new puppy while he went out. He hadn't had it very long, and he didn't want to leave it alone all day. Josh and Ellie needed some pocket money, too. **// (change of place)** At the cricket club, Mr Knight was busy talking to the team captain.

2. There are lots of possible answers to this question. You should be able to explain clearly what the topic of each paragraph is.

3. Any suitable explanation about why it's important to arrange your writing in paragraphs.
   Example:
   Arranging your writing in paragraphs makes it easier for the reader to follow. It keeps events organised in a logical way as well as making dialogue easier to follow.

Pages 52 and 53 — Paragraphs and Subheadings

1. A letter to the head teacher, complaining about homework — no subheadings
   A recount of a school trip — subheadings
   A funny poem — no subheadings
   An adventure story — no subheadings
   A report about African animals and birds — subheadings
   A note to your friend about a party — no subheadings
   A newspaper report — subheadings
   A recipe for scones — subheadings
   A fairy tale — no subheadings
   A write-up of a science experiment — subheadings

2. Any suitable answer.
   Example:
   Why Do People Have Pets?
   There are lots of possible answers to this question.
   Example:
   Make sure your pet has plenty of food and water each day. You should also check that their cage (if they have one) is clean and has things for them to interact with. If you have a dog, it's important to give it plenty of exercise — you should take it for regular walks.

3. There are lots of possible answers to this question.
   Example:
   Choosing the Right Pet
   Choosing the right pet can be difficult. Some pets need a lot of care and attention and can also be expensive to look after. In addition, not every pet will be suitable for your lifestyle. If you're away from home a lot, it wouldn't be a good idea to get a dog or a cat. However, you could consider getting a goldfish.

Answers

Answers

End of Punctuation Quiz

Pages 54 and 55

1. A **F**rench player called **A**ntoine joined **L**iverpool **F**ootball **C**lub, but he had to learn **E**nglish to understand the manager.
   [1 mark for all six correct]

2. In the dark forest**,** a goblin prodded the contents of a cauldron**.** **H**e wore a leather waistcoat and trousers made from an old potato sack**.** **A**s he stirred the mixture**,** it gave off a stench of rotten eggs.
   [1 mark for all seven correct]

3. At two o'clock**,** Chris Jones**,** Erica and Harvey will arrive.
   Add the chopped tomatoes**,** onion and garlic to the pan.
   Recently**,** I have begun to play board games with my sister.
   [2 marks for all 4 commas correct, 1 mark if you got 2 or 3 correct]

4. I don't think it's ready yet. — **C**
   James' room is untidy. — **P**
   Is that your dad's car? — **P**
   The fox's tail was fluffy. — **P**
   The fly's wings shimmered. — **P**
   The taxi's late. — **C**
   [1 mark]

5. the bikes of two boys — **the two boys' bikes**
   the shoes of Angus — **Angus's shoes**
   the play of the children — **the children's play**
   [1 mark]

6. "Are the cakes finished?" asked Isla hungrily. **OR**
   "Are the cakes finished?" asked Isla, hungrily.
   [1 mark]
   "Please be careful Kamal," sighed Mum, "or you'll spill your tea." **OR** "Please be careful, Kamal," sighed Mum, "or you'll spill your tea."
   [1 mark]

7. There are lots of possible answers to this question. Examples:
   "Wipe your shoes," said Mrs Anders. "My carpet is new."
   "Wipe your shoes! My carpet is new," said Mrs Anders.
   "My carpet is new, so wipe your shoes!" said Mrs Anders.
   [1 mark]

8. There are lots of possible answers to this question. Examples:
   (its) The mouse got its tail caught in the door.
   (it's) I think it's better to walk to school, if you can.
   [1 mark]

Answers

Spelling
Section 10 — Prefixes

Page 56 — Prefix: 're'

1. Let me **reassure** you: there are no spiders in the bath!
   I had to **remove** the broken tile.
   The archaeologists decided to **re-enter** the tomb.
   We had to **re-cover** the bird's cage when it squawked.

2. Any suitable answer.
   Example:
   repair means **the socks are being mended**.
   re-pair means **the socks are being put back into pairs**.

Page 57 — Prefix: 'auto'

1. **automatic**, **autocue**, **automobile**, **autobiography**, **autograph**

2. Any suitable answer.
   Example:
   auto**focus** — a device that makes a camera focus itself.
   The photographs came out blurry when I forgot to use the autofocus.

Pages 58 and 59 — Negative Prefixes: 'il', 'im', 'in' and 'ir'

1. il-: **illegal, illogical, illegible**
   im-: **immortal, impatient, impolite, immobile, imbalance**
   in-: **inaccurate, inexpensive, infinite, inconsiderate**
   ir-: **irrelevant, irregular, irresponsible**

2. It was **irresponsible** to balance the antique vase on a wobbly pile of books.
   Some people believe that there are an **infinite** number of stars in the universe.
   The game was **inexpensive**, but the postage was very costly.
   A smear of strawberry jam across the page had made the letter **illegible**.
   Unfortunately, my clock was **inaccurate** and I ended up being fifteen minutes late for the appointment.
   Dad became **impatient** with the man counting out his change at the checkout.

3. There are lots of possible answers to this question.
   Examples:
   The prefix 'il-' is added to words that begin with the letter **'l'**. An example of this is **'illegal'**.
   The prefix 'im-' is added to words that begin with the letters **'m'**, **'p'** and **'b'**. An example of this is **'imbalance'**.
   The prefix 'ir-' is added to words that begin with the letter **'r'**. An example of this is **'irresponsible'**.

Page 60 — Prefixes: 'anti' and 'multi'

1. **anti**social, **anti**septic, **multi**national, **multi**lingual, **anti**freeze, **multi**coloured.

2. Jane worked for a huge **multinational** company.
   The vet used **antiseptic** to prevent infection.
   Go away! I'm feeling **antisocial**.
   The explosion at the paint factory left the walls **multicoloured**.

3. Any suitable answer.
   Examples:
   anti**dote** — a medicine to work against a poison.
   multi**tasking** — doing many different things at once.

Section 11 — Word Endings and Suffixes

Page 61 — Suffixes: 'ous'

1. **glamorous, disastrous, ambitious, marvellous, courageous, suspicious**

2. We walked **anxiously** down the **perilous** path.
   There were **poisonous** toadstools along the path, and a **mysterious** light shone from the abbey.

Pages 62 and 63 — Suffixes: 'shun' / 'zhun' endings

1. -tion: **reaction, direction, collection, demonstration, completion**
   -sion: **decision, confusion, explosion, extension, persuasion**
   -ssion: **possession, transmission, confession, expression**
   -cian: **politician, magician, mathematician, electrician, optician, logician**

2. musician, electrician, mathematician, magician, optician, politician, technician

3. **admission, division, protection, conclusion**s

Answers

4. Any suitable sentences.
   Examples:
   I got lost on holiday and had to ask for **directions**.
   Marc didn't finish his work on time so he got an **extension**.
   Take all your **possessions** with you.

Pages 64 and 65 — Suffixes: Syllables and Doubling Consonants

1. ad — mi — ra — tion
   fea — ther
   a — ni — mal
   ma — the — ma — ti — cal
   (You may have split the word slightly differently, but the words should be split into the same number of syllables as shown above.)

2. You should have underlined:
   pr<u>o</u>mise, <u>o</u>ver, <u>e</u>nter, negl<u>e</u>ct, r<u>e</u>main, chil<u>d</u>ren

3. Any suitable sentences.
   Examples:
   sus<u>p</u>ect: Ben was the **suspect** in the robbery.
   sus<u>pe</u>ct: I **suspect** that someone ate my lunch.
   <u>pre</u>sent: They bought me a lovely **present**.
   pre<u>se</u>nt: They decided to **present** him with an award.

4. Any suitable sentences.
   Examples:
   garden — ✗ + er = gardener (or gardening, gardened)
   occur — ✓ + ed = occurred (or occurring)
   begin — ✓ + ing = beginning (or beginner)
   visit — ✗ + ed = visited (or visiting)

5. Any suitable sentences.
   Examples:
   I would like to be a **gardener** and spend lots of time outside.
   The party was just **beginning** when I got there.

Page 66 — Word Endings: 'ture', 'sure', 'gue' and 'que'

1. **pleasure, antique, mixture, colleague, league, leisure, adventure, dialogue**

2. The Black Death was a terrible pla**gue**.
   You'll get pla**que** if you don't clean your teeth twice a day.
   The x-ray showed that my arm had a frac**ture**.
   You'll have to mea**sure** to see if it will fit.
   I don't know exactly, but I have a va**gue** idea.
   The teacher showed great displea**sure** when I failed my test.

Section 12 — Confusing Words

Page 67 — Words Containing 'sc' Making An 's' Sound

1. fa**sc**inating
   de**sc**end
   ad**olesc**ent
   scenery
   di**sc**i**pl**ine

2. **sc**ience — Physics, chemistry or biology
   scent — Smell or odour
   a**sc**end — Climb or rise up
   scissors — A tool for cutting things

Pages 68 and 69 — Tricky Homophones

1. circled: course, saw
   The material was **coarse** and made his skin **sore**.
   circled: loan, night, road
   The **lone knight rode** out to battle.
   circled: piece, cymbal
   The protester drew a **peace symbol** on the wall.
   circled: their, plain, stair
   There was nothing to do on the **plane** but **stare** out of the window.

2. The **throne** was moved into the palace.
   When the window broke, we all looked at the girl who had **thrown** the ball.

3. Any suitable drawings.
   The first should show an island with baked beans/ supermarket shelves on it.
   The second should show a moose made from strawberries.
   The third should show chickens/ducks/geese during a football match.

Page 70 — Unstressed and Silent Vowels

1. unstressed <u>a</u>: **diction<u>a</u>ry, station<u>a</u>ry, calend<u>a</u>r**
   unstressed <u>e</u>: **gen<u>e</u>rous, diff<u>e</u>r<u>e</u>nce** (either or both 'e' may be underlined), **gen<u>e</u>ral, int<u>e</u>resting**
   unstressed <u>i</u>: **parl<u>i</u>ament, bus<u>i</u>ness**
   unstressed <u>o</u>: **hist<u>o</u>ry, choc<u>o</u>late, fact<u>o</u>ry**

2. **aband<u>o</u>ned, defin<u>i</u>tely, sep<u>a</u>rate, orig<u>i</u>nally**

Answers

Pages 71, 72 and 73 — Words from the Year 3/4 Spelling List

1. What you've written for this depends on which words you know.

2. You should have circled: accidentally, different, business, naughty, disappear, grammar, actually, weight.

3. The children **accidentally** spilt water on the carpet.
   "I have made your doughnut **disappear**," said Tim, brushing sugar from his mouth.
   It's **naughty** to run in school — except in an emergency.
   What's in my diary is none of your **business**.

4. You should have crossed out and corrected:
   strenth — **strength**
   rain — **reign**
   medecine — **medicine**
   presure — **pressure**

5. Any suitable underlining.
   Examples:
   fav<u>ou</u>rite, h<u>ea</u>rd, pec<u>u</u>liar, qu<u>ar</u>ter

6. library, surprise, exercise, interest, height, particular, ordinary, occasional, experience, century, sentence, regular

End of Spelling Quiz

Pages 74 and 75

1. The teacher had to **re-mark** the test.
   I **resent** having to send a thank-you card.
   [1 mark]

2. against the law — **illegal**
   cannot be done — **impossible**
   not on the subject — **irrelevant**
   childish — **immature**
   [1 mark]

3. courage — **courageous**
   continue — **continuous**
   religion — **religious**
   fame — **famous**
   fury — **furious**
   anxiety — **anxious**
   [1 mark]

4. decide — **decision**
   magic — **magician**
   collide — **collision**
   explode — **explosion**
   compete — **competition**
   admit — **admission**
   music — **musician**
   suspect — **suspicion**
   [2 marks for all words correct, or 1 mark if you got five, six or seven correct]

5. You should have underlined the following words: preferred, beginning, gardener, labelled, limited, travelled, happening, preferable
   [1 mark]

6. ack-see-dent — **accident**
   sur-tun — **certain**
   o-kay-shun-ally — **occasionally**
   nor-tee — **naughty**
   op-o-set — **opposite**
   se-pur-ut — **separate**
   [2 marks for all words correct, or 1 mark if you got four or five correct]

7. eaglue = **league**, quineu = **unique**, squome = **mosque**, gufatie = **fatigue**
   [1 mark]

8. Pippa left the supermarket ~~isle~~ (**aisle**) and stood in the ~~cue~~ (**queue**).
   The ~~cymbal~~ (**symbol**) on the ~~rode~~ (**road**) sign showed there was no way ~~threw~~ (**through**).
   My dog will ~~stair~~ (**stare**) at a ~~peace~~ (**piece**) of cake until he is given ~~sum~~ (**some**).
   [1 mark for correctly giving all the words shown above in brackets]

Answers

End of Book Test

Pages 76-81

1. A tick should be placed next to the third sentence: "Leave the door open," said Kim, "while I go outside." *[1 mark]*

2. **We** visit the same beach every summer. **It** doesn't get too busy and there's a lovely café there. *[1 mark]*

3. You should have underlined 'on the other side of the football pitch'.
   There are lots of fronted adverbials you could have written. For example:
   Straight after the sack race
   [1 mark]

4. You should have underlined 'Because it was her mother's birthday'.
   There are lots of expanded noun phrases that you could have written. For example:
   a beautiful bunch of flowers
   [1 mark]

5. Charlie took (some) pens, but they were mine, not his. *[1 mark]*

6. simple past: **charged, bumped, yelled, were**
   past progressive: **wasn't looking, was going**
   present perfect: **I've hurt**
   [1 mark]

7. There are lots of possible answers to this question. Example:
   Since it was Ethan's birthday, Ben made a cake, but he burnt it. *[1 mark]*

8. Before he arrived, we **were** locked in the house.
   OR: Before he **arrives**, we are locked in the house.
   [1 mark]

9. **im**possible, **ir**responsible, **in**secure, **il**legal, **im**mortal, **in**credible *[1 mark]*

10. The word 'Noah's' should be circled.
    [1 mark]

11. ten**sion**, electri**cian**, men**tion**, elec**tion**, man**sion**, mi**ssion**, po**tion**, musi**cian**, confu**sion** *[1 mark]*

12. **Without** looking, he stepped out into the road.
    With an evil chuckle, Harriet closed the lid.
    I can't go on Tuesday. I've got to go to Liverpool.
    OR: I can't go on Tuesday: I've got to go to Liverpool. OR: I can't go on Tuesday; I've got to go to Liverpool.
    [1 mark]

13. **Planting seeds is fun. Each type of seed develops in a different number of days. When the young plants have four leaves, you can put them in bigger pots.** *[1 mark]*
    You can write the second sentence as: **When the young plant has four leaves, you can put it in a bigger pot.**

14. Rover chased a squirrel up the tallest oak tree in the park while barking enthusiastically.
    [1 mark]

15. You should have circled the following words: happiness, tension, hope, stupidity, luck *[1 mark]*

16. Mum gave Dan and **me** a choice of rewards.
    Bobby and **I** asked if we could go out.
    [1 mark]

17. There are lots of possible answers to this question. Example: **so he had something to do** on the train.
    [1 mark]

18. The **children's** playground was full of noise.
    I listened to the **singer's** solo.
    We returned the **child's** toy to her mother.
    The conductor checked the **singers'** costumes.
    [1 mark]

19. You should have circled the following words: surprise, occasion, calendar, accidentally *[1 mark]*

20. There are lots of possible words you can add to the sentence. Example:
    Everybody was jealous of Tina's **new** pencil case.
    Word class: **adjective**. *[1 mark]*

21. You should have underlined the following words: happily and almost. *[1 mark]*

22. When swans are disturbed, they can become violent. *[1 mark]*

23. The paragraph break should be placed as shown:
    ...go back to school. // In the morning... *[1 mark]*

24. I should **have** seen the doctor earlier.
    Tim and **I weren't** sure which was the **best** way to go.
    [1 mark]

25. "My car won't start**,**" said Amy**, "**and the garage is closed." *[1 mark]*